Growing Up to the Head

Ten Growth Essentials to
Becoming a Better Christian

The Role and Responsibility
of Every Christian in Church Growth

Books Written
by the Author

Faithful Over a Few Things:	
Seven Critical Church Growth Principles	$19.95
Faithful Over a Few Things Study Guide	$ 9.95
Breaking the Huddle	$14.95
Growing Up to the Head:	
Ten Growth Essentials to Becoming a Better Christian	$19.95
Growing Up to the Head Workbook	$10.95
Praising the Hell Out of Yourself	$19.95
Praising the Hell Out of Yourself Workbook	$11.95
Stir Up the Gifts	$24.95
Stir Up the Gifts:	
New and Improved Workbook and Study Guide	$10.95
Stir Up the Gifts Leader's Guide	$10.95
Sin in the House	$19.95
How to Be Blessed	$19.95
A Good Black Samaritan	$4.95

All books may be ordered individually or in quantity. Prices do not include shipping and handling costs. Discounts are available for purchases in quantity.

To place an order, call toll-free: (800) 561-0439, or (770) 808-0999. You may fax your order 24-hours a day, seven days a week to (770) 808-1955. You may also e-mail your order to Ormanmcc@aol.com or mail your order to the following address:

Orman Press, Inc.
4200 Sandy Lake Drive
Lithonia, Georgia 30038

GROWING UP
to the
HEAD

Ten Growth Essentials
to Becoming a Better Christian

By
George O. McCalep Jr., Ph.D.

The Role and Responsibility
of Every Christian in Church Growth

Growing Up
to the
Head

Copyright © 1997

Orman Press
Lithonia, Georgia
ISBN 0-9652262-3-9
All Rights Reserved
Printed in the United States of America

DEDICATION

I would like to dedicate *Growing Up to the Head* to the members of the Greenforest Community Baptist Church, who, over the last eighteen years, have submitted themselves to individual and collective spiritual growth.

It is because of their commitment to spiritual maturity and discipleship that our congregation has grown from a mission status of twenty-five members to a fully-autonomous family of 4,500 active members.

I am thankful that they have grown in their love for God to the point that they trust Him, me and the entire leadership team, as demonstrated by their will to constantly change or do whatever is necessary to advance the Kingdom and the family of God.

ACKNOWLEDGEMENTS

First and always giving all praise and glory to God, I acknowledge His lead and His presence in the writing of this book.

Second, I want to acknowledge my wife of thirty-six years, Sadie, for her patience and for the hours of quality prime time that were borrowed from our family.

I want to acknowledge the work of my three editors: Olivia M. Cloud for her gift of manuscript development and book production; Karlene Crawford for her solid, challenging theological perspective; and Susan Smith for her creative editing and her production of the study sections.

I also want to thank Rev. Elgia Wells for asking me to teach the Book of Ephesians at a leadership conference that eventually led to the writing of this book.

TABLE
of
CONTENTS

FOREWORD

My good friend George McCalep has written a church growth book that breaks new and refreshing ground. It is about growing people. He gives ten practical and biblical principles for "Becoming a Better Christian." George argues convincingly from Scripture and practice that congregational spiritual growth is the key to church numerical growth. If you have grown weary of church growth books that seem more attuned to Madison Avenue than Scriptural principles, you are going to find this book refreshing.

This is a new and much-needed approach to church growth. George finds his ten essentials for spiritual growth in the Ephesian letter. I have often said that the Bible is the church growth manual and that Ephesians is the key letter about the authority of the church. George has taken Paul's letter to the Ephesians seriously and applied it practically to the church today. This book is not simply a book for pastors to read about church growth. It is a workbook for the church member to read about spiritual growth.

George not only deals with the biblical texts, he concludes every chapter with application questions that will lead to productive discussion which could help facilitate church growth. He gives practical helps for believers, such as his seven keys to everlasting joy or his three stages of growing in grace. George's ten essentials for growth address such issues as reconciliation, prayer, love, behavior, the fullness of the Holy Spirit, and spiritual strength. I appreciate his honesty. He deals with the hard issues, such as racial reconciliation and holy living, that are often omitted in the name of church growth. His illustrations and conclusions are hard-hitting.

While George often illustrates from his African-American perspective, this book can be used by any congregation, with great merit. You may not agree with everything that George says. You will be challenged in your thinking patterns; you will not be the same when you finish. George challenges the reader to grow. His clear declaration in the introduction sets the pace for this challenging work. "His purpose should be our purpose. Until His purpose becomes our purpose, we are still children with the need to grow up to the fullness of Christ." George calls God the divine Architect who has made plans to build up His highest creation according to what needs to be done. The Architect has a plan and purpose for all His creations.

What makes this book even more powerful is the living model that stands behind it—the Greenforest Community Baptist Church in Decatur, Georgia. I had the privilege of visiting this great church when I was the director of the Southern Baptist Center for Church Growth. Here is a church that practices what its pastor preaches! It is a church that has grown from mission status to a fellowship of more than 4,500 as individual Christians have grown in faith and lived out that faith in their community.

Read it! Study it! Respond to it! See what God will do in your life.

Kenneth S. Hemphill, D.Min., Ph.D.
President
Southwestern Baptist Theological Seminary

A Call for Collective Numerical Growth Through Individual Spiritual Growth

WHICH COMES FIRST—THE "GO" OR THE "MAKE"?

It is the Christian duty of every believer to grow. Growth is a normal process of an organism, and the Church is an organ-

A full house on Sunday morning can be the result of members growing up in the fullness of Christ.

ism. The church cannot grow unless the members of the church grow. The reason many churches are not growing numerically is because the members are not growing spiritually. A full house on Sunday morning can be the result of members growing up in the fullness of Christ. If filling the house numerically were the main objective, all we would need to do is build smaller houses (churches).

Based on Scriptural interpretation of "The Great Commission," a theological issue can be raised here. Which came first in The Great Commission, the "go" or the "make"? Many feel this is as trivial as the question, Which came first, the chicken or the egg? I am persuaded, however, that a misunderstanding and misinterpretation has led to a decline in church growth. In other words, churches are not growing because of this misunderstanding. Misinterpretation leads to misdirection and misbehavior. I am not a Greek scholar, yet we have been told for years that the Greek text should be interpreted, "As you are going, make disciples." Based on this simple, informed interpretation, it can be easily determined that the word "make" is the only word of command in The Great Commission. In the Greek, the verbs "go," "baptize," and "teach" are actually in participle form.

God said to me, "You have been recruiting Christians and not making disciples."

The instruction is clear: "make disciples." Make disciples and they will go. Yet, most of our evangelistic literature begins with the emphasis on "go." I have heard pastor after pastor refer to the front end of The Great Commission as the "go" and the back end as the "make." We have the cart before the horse. We're not emphasizing where God told us to start. According to our literature and behavior, this is a universal church growth problem.

God first touched my heart on this matter several years ago at a leadership conference in Ridgecrest, NC. I had been pastoring for about fourteen years, and the church where I serve as pastor had experienced tremendous growth—from about twenty-five members to about 2,000 at that time. (Our present active membership is over 4,500.) The message God gave me was as clear and compelling as was my call to preach. The message was not only clear, it was convicting. God said to me, "You have been recruiting Christians and not making disciples."

My thought was, "But God, what about numbers?" God replied, "I want you to first make disciples." I told my wife and congregation about my message from God. They were sympathetic. My wife tried to comfort me by telling me what a good job I had done over the past fourteen years. Yet, God was still saying, "You're really not doing what I want you to do. You've got the 'go' in front of the 'make.' I want you to put the 'make' in front of the 'go.'" God said, "Make disciples and then they will go."

"... when we do authentic discipleship, evangelism will follow."

At this point I began to study the way I did church and the way most of our churches do church. I discovered that most of us seem to be doing church backwards. We say that when we do evangelism, we must also do discipleship. We admit that discipleship must accompany evangelism. But that's not the whole truth. The whole truth is that when we do authentic discipleship, evangelism will follow. The first duty of a disciple is to "go." I also discovered that much of our Sunday School literature is written as if "go" were the command verb in The Great Commission.

In the secular world, we've heard a lot about establishing new paradigms—new ways of looking at or approaching various tasks and organizational structures. For most of us, what I am suggesting is a different approach. It really isn't a new paradigm. For me, it is simply fresh inspiration on the established revelation given by Jesus in His last earthly instructions to the Church: "As you are going and before you go, make disciples."

A filled people produce a full house. Fill the people and they will fill the house.

As previously mentioned, the only command verb in The Great Commission is "make." A disciple will and must "go." If we grow the congregation up to the fullness and likeness of Christ, they will go. Evangelism is not an option for a mature Christian, regardless of his or her gifts. In the parable of the great banquet, Jesus said, "Go out into the highways and hedges and compel them to come in, that my house may be filled." Jesus desires a full house. *A filled people produce a full house.* Fill the people, and they will fill the house.

Grow them up to the Head so that His fullness may be their fullness and the numerical membership will increase. Mature, grown up Christians produce numerically filled churches. Grow the congregation up to the Head and God's house will be numerically full. Again, if filling the house numerically is the goal, we should all simply build smaller structures.

When considering the issue of growth, there are concerns for both clergy and laity. Growth (whether spiritual or numerical) is not simply the responsibility of the pastor. The questions this book proposes to laypersons (church members) are, "Do you want to grow? Do you want to be all God would have you to be?"

The question proposed to pastors and other church leaders is, "Do you want your church to grow numerically?" If the answer is yes, then you must first encourage your members to grow spiritually. Spiritual growth requires growing up into His fullness.

THE INSPIRATION

I taught one of the Bible study lectures from the biblical exposition course on the Book of Ephesians during Black Church Leadership Week '96, at Ridgecrest Conference Center in North Carolina. The lectures were converted, with many direct quotations, into an article printed in the September 5, 1996, issue of *The Christian Index.* The article and message were entitled "Tearing Down the Walls." I have received numerous phone calls, letters and faxes from people across the country thanking me for the blessing and encouraging me to continue on my mission

Growing Up to the Head is about the relationship of congregational spiritual growth to church numerical growth.

of reconciliation, perfecting the church, and Kingdom building. A special letter of encouragement came by letter from Dr. Larry Lewis, then president of the Home Mission Board of the Southern Baptist Convention (now the North American Mission Board).

Under the anointing of the Holy Spirit, I was then challenged and inspired by God to put into print what God had revealed to me concerning "growing up to the Head: which is the role and responsibility of each and every church member."

Inspiration for this book also came from a void that was identified from the study of the book I authored entitled *Faithful Over a Few Things: Seven Critical Church Growth Principles* (Orman Press, 1996), which is based on three basic assumptions:

1. The pastor is the chief catalyst in church growth
2. There is but so much time in a day; therefore, what the

pastor can do is limited

3. If the church and her leadership do a few things well, God will grow His Church

Based on these assumptions, the question was raised, "Is there a book designed for the average church member?" *Growing Up to The Head* is designed to help the average church member, as well as pastors and church leaders, participate in the ministry of church growth. *Growing Up to the Head* is about the relationship of congregational spiritual growth to church numerical growth.

This book stresses that individual spiritual growth is a precursor to meaningful numerical church growth. In other words, where there is spiritual growth there will also be numerical growth. However, it is possible for a church to experience numerical growth without spiritual growth because many people simply desire to be entertained. Spiritual growth yields much deeper levels of church growth. Growing up is about the role and responsibility of every Christian to church growth. *Growing Up to the Head* can be considered a church growth book for laymen.

GROWING UP TO THE HEAD

The Body of Christ

The Church is defined as the body of Christ. Christ is the perfect Head. What happens when the body of Christ does not match the Head? The same conflict

> *But speaking the truth in love, may grow up into him in all things, which is the head, even Christ.* **Ephesians 4:15**

and sense of incompleteness which dwells in a person who has not grown up to the Head can also be present within the body of Christ. Certain conditions and telltale signs are present among individuals who are experiencing conflict in their relationship with God. The same can be true of a church.

The local body which is too small for the Head is a church that operates with a small spirit—and small faith. If they had grown up to the Head, they could see the great potential to do Kingdom work. It doesn't matter about the numerical size of the congregation. Large congregations can be small (or poor) in spirit.

When a local body has not grown up to the Head, its members may give sparingly—causing the church to rely on gimmicks in order to keep the church afloat financially. When the body is too small, the church may feel there's nothing wrong with the fact that no one has joined or been bap-

A local body of believers must continually strive to grow up to the Head.

tized in their church for as long as anyone can remember.

Members of a church body that is disproportionate to the Head see nothing wrong with the fact that their church is only open for Sunday School, worship, Bible study and choir rehearsal. Immorality may abound within such a body because everyone (perhaps including the pastor) takes the attitude that "I'm grown and what I do is my own business."

As it is with people, churches must also "grow up." A local body of believers must continually strive to grow up to the Head. We cannot be perfect, neither as individuals nor as churches. What we can do, however, is to understand what Christ desires of us and to make His desire our standard for life.

Just think, how could the body of a six-month-old baby support the head of an adult male? Imagine how frustrating that would be for both the body and the head! The head is thinking mature thoughts and making adult plans and decisions. Yet the body is too weak to support what the head wants to do. In the same way, how can a weak or fragile

...how can a weak or fragile church body support the work set forth by its Head?

church body support the work set forth by its Head? Christ has great plans for His church. Yet those plans cannot be carried out by a body that is too small in faith, in deed and in spirit. How can a body so small even understand the workings of a Head that is too big for it? Christ equipped the body with everything needed, just as human beings are given everything needed at birth. Still, a growth process must take place.

This book is about the ministry of the body (congregation). Ministry comes from the body (church members). Leadership comes from the pastor. Pastors should read this book so they can better understand and lead the ministry of the body. Members should read this book so that they may grow up to do the ministry of the church. When this happens, the pastor can be loosed to carry out the responsibilities of leadership.

FROM RIDICULE TO RESPECT

Over the years, I have discovered that the source of my dismay in my youth has become the source of my blessing. When I was a boy, my head was disproportionately larger than the rest of my body. The nature of children being what it is, I was often teased about the size of my head. My head was the source of constant ridicule, and I was probably called every "head" name a child's imagination could conceive. People referred to me as a "big headed" little boy. Other children and adults would poke fun at me because of my head. People can be cruel. I was called names like "flat head" or "big head" or "wopsey." My head also prevented me from being swift, agile, and mobile. When I would attempt to run fast, leaning backward, my big head would pull me too far back; or, if I attempted to lean forward, my head would pull me forward and I would fall on my face. The problem was that my head was out of proportion to my body. Thank

God I am no longer a big head with a little body. My body finally caught up with my head.

I didn't know it then, but that very same source of ridicule would later be a source of glory. As I grew older, my body caught up with my head. People were unconcerned with the size of my head. They began to compliment my intellect. Then when my hair began to turn gray, people began to compliment its natural beauty.

Those days of ridicule are long gone, but living through the experience helped to enhance my spiritual growth. When my body grew up to my head, I did not—could not—forget the journey. Part of that growth was a painful process. But now that my head and body are proportionate in size, I recognize a complete person when I look in the mirror. No one part seems out of place.

My head is no longer the subject of ridicule nor the cause of low self-esteem. Rather, my head (fully covered with natural, God-grown white hair)

The Head is perfect, but the church has really not become His glory.

is now the subject of my positive God-esteem. God grew my body out to my head and crowned it for His glory. As I see the church today, the body is grossly out of proportion, and the Head is not being crowned by the body. The Head is perfect, but the church has really not become His glory.

When we are not in proper relationship with God, it is as though the body ("us") has not grown up to the Head (God). We can never feel whole and complete as long as the body is so much smaller than the Head. Something always feels out of sync. Something looks out of place.

INTO HIS FULLNESS

Paul, in the Book of Ephesians, refers to mature Christians as being in the "fullness of Christ" and the immature Christians as "babes in Christ." In my opinion, all of us are "babes," with the need to grow up to the "fullness of Christ."

The church that I have been blessed and privileged to pastor for the last eighteen years has as its motto, "A Church With the Richness and Fullness of the Presence of JESUS." In my opinion, this is what the church should strive to become: a community where the richness of His fullness is present. I feel that this is what God had in mind when He inspired the Apostle Paul to mention four times in the Book of Ephesians, "the fullness of God." Ephesians 1:10, 23; 3:19; 4:13.

Speaking of the church, God tells us in Ephesians 1:22-23, "And hath put all things under his feet, and gave him to be the head over all things to the church, Which is his body, the fullness of him that filleth all in all." Simply put, Christ is perfect and complete and is the Head of all, especially His church, which is His body. Therefore, the body is not the facility in which the believers gather. The church is not brick and mortar and stained-glass windows. Neither is the church a social or religious institution. The Church is the fullness of God; the body made up of baptized believers. We are the church.

The Church is the fullness of God; the body made up of baptized believers. We are the church.

Many years ago, while doing some door-to-door evangelism in a community near our church, an irate man came to the door when I rang the doorbell. I told him the nature of my call, and he immediately told me that he did not believe in organized religion. He was somewhat dumbfounded when I immediately told him that I did not believe in organized religion either.

The church is not supposed to be an organized religious institution. The church is the body of Christ. We, the believers, make up that body. Therefore, believers, both individually and collectively, are to grow up in His fullness. This book, *Growing Up to the Head*, is about growing up into His fullness. Growing into His fullness is to strive to become like Him; to

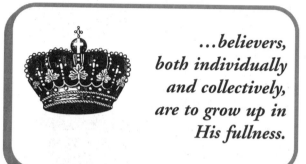

...believers, both individually and collectively, are to grow up in His fullness.

walk in His steps. Growing up into His fullness means to join Him in His agenda. Growing up into His fullness means to daily walk after Him. Growing up into His fullness means to become full to the brim with His teachings and His love. Growing up into His fullness means to let your cup run over with His praise and His joy and His spiritual blessings.

John 15:11 states, "These things have I spoken unto you, that my joy might remain in you, and that your joy might be full." Growing up into His fullness means becoming joyfully full. Growing up into His fullness means becoming all He would have you to be. Growing up into His fullness means having the mind of Christ and doing the will of Christ. Colossians 1:9b states, "... to desire that ye might be filled with the knowledge of his will in all wisdom and spiritual understanding."

God has blessed my wife, Sadie, and me with three sons whom we love very much. Our 33-year-old son, who bears my name, George, lost 99.99% of his hearing as a result of spinal meningitis, with the associated high fever, which burned and severed the nerve connected to the ear. Because of his deafness, our family has had to learn sign language as a means of communication. One of the signs that always strikes me as interesting is the sign for full. With your hand in a palm down position, you move your hand from your waist to under your chin, indicating that you are full. In other words, the body is filled up to the head.

God is calling us, the body of Christ, to be filled up to the Head. God is calling His church to grow up. God is calling every believer to grow up. Too many Christians have

God is calling us, the body of Christ, to be filled up to the Head. God is calling His church to grow up.

become stunted in their growth. Far too many Christians are still on milk and infant formula. Far too many adults are still wearing spiritual diapers. Far too many church members have not put down their spiritual baby bottles. God has admonished each and every one of us to grow up into His fullness. Ephesians 4:13 tells us that we should continue to grow "till we all come in the unity of the faith, and of the knowledge of the Son of God, unto a perfect man, unto the measure of the stature of the fullness of Christ." We, therefore, are challenged to grow up into His fullness—to grow up to the perfect Head.

COMING INTO PERFECTION

The world's church critics have drawn a picture of a church with a little body and a big head. The world is poking fun at the church for her inability to make good on God's promises. The

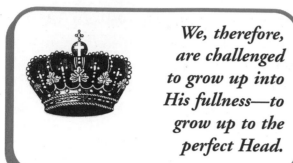

We, therefore, are challenged to grow up into His fullness—to grow up to the perfect Head.

problem is that the body is weak. The body is anemic.

It must be remembered that the body is only as strong as her members. Likewise, the human body is only as strong as its parts. When the physical body is weak, it must be strengthened. When the church body is weak, her members need strengthening. Her members need spiritual growth. Too many pastors and church leaders are trying to grow the church from without rather than from within. Growth from the outside can be deceptive. It can be impressive, leading the pastor and the membership into thinking that everything is fine and that everyone is doing a fantastic job.

A few years ago, the cover of *Essence* magazine featured a beautiful young woman. She appeared to be the embodiment of health and vitality. Any man would have been proud to claim her as his wife. But the picture of the woman did not reveal the entirety of her condition. The young woman was also HIV positive. She knew that someday she would die of AIDS. Yet, in that photograph, no one could look at her and know that.

Sometimes churches are unhealthy, yet appear to be the picture of health and vitality. They may have large memberships, massive edifices, and televised services—yet they are sick on a level which is not readily visible. Eventually, the unhealthy parts of the membership will manifest. Often, when a crisis situation develops in such churches, the pastor, the leaders and the members are poorly equipped to handle the problem because of the low level of spiritual maturity within the body.

The problem of the church lies within the church and her membership. Many churches seek numerical, external growth. Growth from the outside produces superficial growth, but growth from within produces permanent growth. Spiritual growth will result in numerical growth. Spiritual growth must take place in the hearts and lives of individual members.

SPIRITUAL MATURITY VS. BEING SPIRITUAL

Again, this book is not only for church leaders, but particularly for the average church member. Brother and Sister Average Church Member must grow up spiritually for the church to grow up to the Head. Growing up spiritually means becoming spiritually mature.

Being spiritually mature means not being unstable and easily deceived by false doctrine. Being spiritually mature means having a clear focus relative to the purpose of the church and the role of the believer, according to the word and will of God. Many believers today seem to be very spiritual, but are not spiritually mature. Many travel from one uplifting

Many believers today seem to be very spiritual, but are not spiritually mature.

spiritual conference to another. Many practice "quiet time" or "devotion time" and have long periods of meditation—becoming more and more spiritual—and yet are not spiritually mature. All the aforementioned are well and good and should continue to be encouraged. However, being spiritually mature means doing God's will relative to the purpose of the (body of Christ) church. Being spiritually mature means being actively involved in helping the body grow up to the Head.

Believers remain children when their understanding of the truth of God's agenda in Christ remains inadequate. God in Christ is purposeful and intentional, and unless the believer joins the purpose and intention, he/she remains an immature child. God's truth is rooted in love. The believer's love is first directed to Christ, then to the body of Christ, and then to each other. Failure to do all three leaves the believer incomplete and not yet grown up to the fullness of Christ.

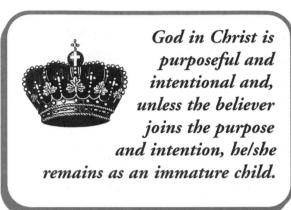

God in Christ is purposeful and intentional and, unless the believer joins the purpose and intention, he/she remains as an immature child.

In order to grow in the fullness of Christ, the church and her leadership must actively seek to present the church according to the truth of Scripture. This means proclaiming the truth in love over loyalty to culture, tradition, and the Christian religious institution. Therefore, changes must occur. But these changes must begin inside, not only with the heart but also by the renewing of the mind relative to our purpose. His purpose should be our purpose. Until His purpose becomes our purpose, we are still children with the need to grow up to the fullness of Christ.

It must be recognized that change—both for individuals and institutions—is very difficult. It is sad to believe that some Christians do not wish to see others grow spiritually. Some churches do not want their pastor to lead the membership toward spiritual growth. There are many people who accept the status quo. They are perfectly happy with things staying just the way they are because "that's the way we've always done it."

Some believers, when confronted with the need for personal growth and development, resist with a vengeance. So many people run away from spiritual growth because they

So many people run away from spiritual growth because they do not want to acknowledge their brokenness.

do not want to acknowledge their brokenness. They do not want to acknowledge their personal responsibility to change their spiritual condition. They do not want to yield themselves over to the Lord so that He might "have thine own way."

It is no wonder, then, that many church bodies are anemic. If the individual members are spiritually anemic, then the church body can do no better. A sickly church body will always lag

If the church's leadership is sickly, the church will simply limp along, never growing to its full potential.

pitifully behind the Head. If the pastor and church leaders are anemic, their leadership will be weak and sickly. If the church's leadership is sickly, the church will simply limp along, never growing to its full potential. So many of our churches are in need of spiritual rebirth. Some have never even attempted to grow up to the Head. They are simply dragging along with no change, no growth, no vision. The same thing happens week

Spiritual anemia requires a spiritual boost.

after week. No church can attain a spiritual condition which is greater than that of its members. Spiritual anemia requires a spiritual boost. Ephesians contains some practical truths to conquering spiritual anemia.

Growing Up to the Head is a book on spiritual growth based on the Book of Ephesians, particularly on Ephesians 4:15: "...Speaking the truth in love, may grow up into him in all things, which is the head, even Christ."

GROWING UP TO THE HEAD

In His Everlasting Joy

Ephesians 1:3-14 is actually a doxology. It contains a good deal of instructional information, but it also reveals the author's excitement about the worthiness of God. He's

> **Blessed be the God and Father of our Lord Jesus Christ, who hath blessed us with all spiritual blessings in heavenly places in Christ.**
> **Ephesians 1:3**

excited about what God has done. Likewise, believers must become excited about what God has already done if they are going to become instruments of church growth.

Paul's excitement is an agent for growth in the early church. Paul hardly stops to punctuate his sentences. He's just so excited about God that he just moves through these spiritual blessings. At verse six he stops to speak words of praise about God's glorious grace. Then he talks a little more about how God has blessed His creatures with spiritual blessings. In verse twelve he pauses and says, "… for the praise of his glory." He goes on a little further, and in verse fourteen he says, "To the praise of his glory." The chief aim of man is to know God and enjoy Him in and through the praises of God. God is worthy. He wants and enjoys all of our praise. Growing up in praise includes growing up in His everlasting joy.

Paul clearly understood what it meant to have grown up in everlasting joy. This was a man who was able to sing songs of praise while in jail. In this passage it appears that Paul simply got "caught up" in praising God. He meant to write this portion of the letter to Ephesus in one direction, but he started thinking about the goodness of the Lord. A person who has grown up in the joy that can only come from the Lord can easily get caught up in praise. Have you ever been in conversation with someone and started talking about what the Lord has done for you? Perhaps you didn't even make it back to your original conversation.

Maybe you've been in the midst of a difficult situation. It might have been death, financial ruin, or trouble with your child. When you have grown up in His everlasting joy, somehow, even in the midst of "living hell," you are able to praise the Lord anyhow. The ability to praise God in all circumstances does not come to us automatically. Our human nature does not allow us to praise God at every turn of life.

> *A great part of growing up to the Head involves conforming our nature to that of the Head.*

A great part of growing up to the Head involves conforming our nature to that of the Head. The Apostle Peter explains this growth process in 1 Peter 1:7-9. Suffering and trials, he said, come to prove and refine our faith so that, even though we do not see Christ, we believe in

30

Him and, therefore, "are filled with an inexpressible and glorious joy" (NIV). Part of that growth process includes being able to see the hand of God at work, even in the most difficult circumstances. Anyone can praise God during good times. We must be conformed to the Head in order to praise God in the midst of difficulty.

As excited as Paul is in this text, other Scripture passages demonstrate that it is not uncommon for us to forget to praise God. Matthew 13:44 helps us understand how excited we should be: "Again, the kingdom of heaven is like unto treasure hid in a field; the which when a man hath found, he hideth, and for joy thereof goeth and selleth all that he hath, and buyeth [that field]."

It is good for us to take inventory of the spiritual blessings we have in Christ. The difficulty with spiritual blessings is they sometimes cannot be enumerated like material blessings. And, the sad truth is, we often value material blessings more than spiritual blessings. Growing up in His everlasting joy means placing a greater value on spiritual blessings than anything else.

> *Growing up in His everlasting joy means placing a greater value on spiritual blessings than anything else.*

GROWING OUT OF MATERIALISM

Western culture is very materialistic. The 1980's were often dubbed the "Go-Go '80's" because everyone seemed to be out to acquire and consume for self. Our culture does not give much credence to that which cannot be appraised with a monetary

> *All believers must grow up in everlasting joy to truly appreciate the spiritual blessings of God.*

value. People are quickly impressed if you say, "He is a millionaire." But how many people would take notice of the statement, "She has joy in her soul"? Certainly those who live a life full of luxury yet absent of joy would take notice. In order for believers to become instruments of church growth, they must grow up to appreciate spiritual blessings. All believers must grow up in everlasting joy to truly appreciate the spiritual blessings of God. For this to effectively take place, the believer must first grow out of being rooted in materialism.

Jesus gave repeated warnings about placing the material above the spiritual. In Matthew 6:19, Jesus admonishes us not to place value upon the things which are temporal—the material things which can be taken away from us due to the circumstances of life. Most of us know at least one person who places a high premium on material goods. Have you ever seen such a person lose something of monetary value? It is a terrible sight. I have heard stories of motorists physically attacking other motorists for hitting their automobile.

It is also possible for us to place an unhealthy value on other people. Our children, our spouses, our parents are all only human and bound to disappoint us. When we make another human the seat of our joy, we are sowing the seeds of disappointment.

We must always remember that nothing outside of Christ can bring us joy. People erroneously seek everlasting joy through work, relationships, or materialism. Each of these things can provide a modicum of happiness. The key is that happiness is always temporary and fleeting. This is the fundamental difference between happiness and joy. We can and should get some pleasure from the way we earn a living. Our loved ones will often be a source of happiness which may sometimes be experienced as joy. A new car can give us happiness for a season. Even drug and alcohol use can offer the momentary feeling of happiness. But it must be recognized that all of these are only temporary. We grow weary of our jobs. Our loved ones disappoint us. The new car gets old. The euphoria of a drug or a drink become an addiction which transforms into a prison cell. Growing up to the Head in His everlasting joy means focusing on spiritual blessings rather than material blessings.

Growing up in His everlasting joy does not exclude us from receiving material blessings.

Excursion: God Does Bless Materially

All good and perfect things come from God. Allow me to take you on a brief excursion and praise God for material blessings. I want to remind you that God does bless materially and that it is a wonderful experience because we know it came from Him.

Growing up in His everlasting joy does not exclude us from receiving material blessings. God blesses us all the time. Yet there are some blessings that are so pronounced and profound that they leave a permanent mark on our hearts. For example, when the Summer Olympic games were in Atlanta in 1996, I really wanted to be there. It was really getting to me that the Centennial Olympics were in my city and I didn't have tickets. There were no tickets to be found … no tickets anywhere. But I wanted to go. I even had guests in my house who were participating in the

Olympic track and field events, and I still couldn't get tickets. I tried everything I could to get some tickets. I sought out my good friend who supposedly knew Olympic gold medalist Carl Lewis. I thought he could get me some tickets. He couldn't help me. I used all the leverage and weight I could. I called MARTA (Metro Atlanta Rapid Transit Authority). Since I'm on the MARTA Board, I figured they could get me some tickets. All they could get me was a ride on a crowded bus.

About the time I was ready to give up my search for tickets, I got a letter from a lady I have never seen before. In her letter to me, she mentioned that she is deaf. She lives in California, and her name is Carol Kent Carson. She could not have known previously that I have a grown deaf son. Included with her letter were four tickets to the evening track and field session in the Olympics! I used those tickets to take my sons and my grandson, and together we observed history being made as we sat watching this major Olympic event. God does bless! Every once in a while He just chooses to bless one of His little ones with the desires of the heart for the material things of this world.

As wonderful as material blessings are, if we have grown up in everlasting joy, our desire will be fixed on spiritual blessings. Spiritual blessings are superior to material blessings. We have to take inventory of spiritual blessings.

> *Spiritual blessings are superior to material blessings.*

EPHESUS: A CASE STUDY

The Book of Ephesians provides an excellent case study for the believer who wants to become a vessel of God for kingdom-building in and through personal spiritual growth. Ephesians teaches us that God predestined the Church to grow up to His image. In other words, God wants us to grow up to the Head in His everlasting joy.

Paul wrote the letter to the church at Ephesus from a jail cell in Rome, just as he wrote three other epistles while incarcerated: Philippians, Philemon, and Colossians. I call them the jailhouse epistles. I think it's interesting that a man would write about joy from jail. It's amazing that Paul would write about joy to the church at Philippi while sitting in jail. From a prison cell he wrote the church at Ephesus about being one in the body of Christ, and began it with a praise doxology in which he talks about spiritual blessings in Christ. He didn't write it from a high and lofty place where it's easy to be joyous. Paul had grown up in His everlasting joy. He tells us about the spiritual blessings in Christ in a praise and doxology. He writes it to the church located in the city of Ephesus.

Ephesus was a seaport town, and that does have meaning because anywhere there's a seaport town, whether it's a big city like Miami, or a little city like Portsmouth, Virginia, such towns carry with them some baggage. If it is possible for the water to be crossed, the nature of what comes across the water cannot be controlled. And it's not always the right stuff. Seaport towns don't seek everlasting joy. Theirs is the fleeting pleasure that is rooted in carnality. They are towns with red light districts; towns into which drugs are smuggled. One of the main temples in Ephesus was the Temple of Diana, much like the Temple of Aphrodite in Corinth. All kinds of cultic worship took place in those temples, including prostitution and sexual acts. It was a bad place. These saints who once went to church at the Temple of Diana now came to the church of God at Ephesus. That's why they didn't have any particular problem. (They had cleaned up most of their immoral acts. There is not a lot written about them engaging in immorality.) They had come out of the world into the fullness of Christ.

Some of us should be able to identify with the believers at Ephesus. Most of us Christians no longer go to the places we may have gone before we met Christ. Most of us have given up the night clubs. Most of us have given up the cabaret parties and the BYOB (bring your own bottle) parties. Most of us have given up the Temple of Diana, and we now find our joy in the Lord. We have not grown up in His everlasting joy if we are seeking fulfillment outside of Christ.

> *We have not grown up in His everlasting joy if we are seeking fulfillment outside of Christ.*

In the church at Ephesus, most of the people had cleaned up their lives. Yet there was still a problem in the church: even though they had gotten rid of what was evil and had run out the false apostles and false prophets, they had lost their first love. They weren't doing anything really bad, but they had turned away from their first love. I saw something once that struck my attention and it's still with me. It said, "Good minus God equals Evil." Minus God, there is no such thing as growing up in everlasting joy.

In the Book of Revelation, Chapter 2, we find the root of the problem with the church at Ephesus. The people weren't abnormal. They had not ventured so far away from the Lord that they were unredeemable. In fact, John, writing them from the Isle of Patmos, states the problem quite clearly:

"Unto the angel of the church of Ephesus write; These things saith he that holdeth the seven stars in his right hand, who walketh in the midst of the seven golden candlesticks; I know thy works, and thy labour, and thy patience, and how thou canst not bear them which are evil: and thou hast tried them which say they are apostles, and are not, and hast found them liars: And hast borne, and hast patience, and for my name's sake hast laboured, and hast not fainted. Nevertheless I have somewhat against thee, because thou hast left thy first love. Remember therefore from whence thou art fallen, and repent, and do the first works; or else I will come unto thee quickly, and will remove thy candlestick out of his place, except thou repent."

(Revelation 2:1-5)

"Thou has forgotten thy first love." In other words, John is saying, "You've forgotten who brought you this far. You've forgotten who first loved you. You've forgotten the spiritual blessings that gave you the first hope in your salvation. You have forgotten the only Love that can give you everlasting joy."

> *You've forgotten the spiritual blessings that first gave you the first hope in your salvation.*

They had lost their first love. They were praising God for material blessings more than spiritual blessings. I'm not too sure that's not the way it is with the church today.

Many of us are praising God, but when we say "when the praises go up, the blessings come down," we're thinking about that

Mercedes we've got out in the parking lot. When we say "praises go up, blessings come down," we're thinking about the money we have in our back pocket; the house that we live in and the job that we have—the material blessings that God has bestowed upon us. Growing up in His everlasting joy

Growing up in His everlasting joy means thinking more about the spiritual blessings of God.

means thinking more about the spiritual blessings of God.

We've turned away from our first love. We've turned away from the first hope, the Scripture says, that gave us the everlasting joy of our salvation. We have our minds and our hearts on material blessings, and we're not paying attention or we don't have joy in our hearts for the spiritual blessings God has given us. We live in a world that has grown accustomed to quick fixes. We seek to find joy quickly, such as that which comes from the pursuit of material blessings.

But Paul reminds us that we have spiritual blessings in Christ. The key phrase is "in Christ." The phrase "in Christ" is referenced ten times in this doxology. God pro-

God provides spiritual blessings only in Christ. Separate from Jesus, we cannot expect to have any spiritual blessings.

vides spiritual blessings only in Christ. Separate from Jesus, we cannot expect to have any spiritual blessings. In Christ, I am righteous. In Christ, I am saved. In Christ, I am redeemed. In

Christ, I am forgiven. In Christ, I find that joy and peace that surpasses all understanding. In Christ, I am connected to God the Father. In Christ, I am found faithful. In Christ, I am loved by Him. In Christ, I can raise holy hands that have been in all kinds of places. In Christ, I can call myself a saint. In Christ, my sins, by the blood of Jesus, have been washed away … erased, made clean, only in Christ. That means they no longer exist… gone… wiped out… forgotten. All we have to do then is live in everlasting joy. Praise God for the spiritual blessings we have available to us in Christ.

SEVEN KEYS TO GROWING UP IN EVERLASTING JOY
Count Your Blessings

God, through Paul, gives us (Ephesians 3:1-14) a sevenfold doxology of spiritual blessings, the keys to everlasting joy. When we recognize the true worth of these spiritual blessings, the result is growing up in everlasting joy. They are the kind of blessings that, as the old folks used to say, "I just couldn't keep it to myself." They're the kind you have to tell somebody about.

We think too much about material blessings, and we don't talk enough about spiritual blessings. There are some spiritual blessings we need to concentrate on and praise God for.

SPIRITUAL BLESSING #1
The Joy of Being Chosen

God has chosen us to be holy and blameless (v. 4). He chose me. He chose you. Some of us think that we chose Him, but He chose us. What a joyous blessing it is to be chosen! Have you ever not been chosen? It can affect your sense of worth as a person. Not being chosen (even by another human being), such as on the playground or gymnasium, makes you feel bad. We humans tend to choose the best athlete—the one who is most likely to help our team win.

But think about God. He really doesn't care what you look like, how coordinated you might be, or whether you can run fast or jump high. He doesn't care whether your skin is black, white, red, yellow or brown. He doesn't care whether your hair is kinky, curly or straight. He doesn't care whether you have big feet or little feet or no feet at all. He chose us to be holy and blameless. He did it before the foundation of the world. He predestined it! I don't proclaim to understand fully the doctrine of predestination, but I don't have to—I just believe it. God chose you and He chose me. Those who are in Christ were chosen before the foundation of the world. He knew that you were going to get saved. He knew that you were going to make the decision to believe in Him. That's the first blessing on the journey to everlasting joy. Growing up in His everlasting joy means giving gratitude and praise for simply being chosen.

SPIRITUAL BLESSING #2
The Joy of Adoption

God adopted you and me (Ephesians 1:5-6). When you adopt somebody, you make it legal. If you adopt somebody, it means they share in everything that you have. God adopted us. That means everything the Father has, whether it be the cattle on the hills or His glorious throne, everything that the Father has belongs to you and me. One who has grown up in everlasting joy rejoices over his or her adoption as a child of the Father.

If we can see ourselves as spiritual orphans before God adopted us, we can better appreciate the blessing of adoption. When we understand that God has provided us with an eternal (permanent) home, that represents another step toward growing up in His everlasting joy. If you know much about children who have been adopted, you know that the older children get, the more difficult it is to get them adopted. Older children are usually more grateful to have a permanent home. A newborn will simply assume that a permanent home is a birthright, but not a child who has been tossed around from one foster home to another.

Sin has tossed many of us around from place to place. When we come to understand that because of Christ we now have a permanent home, that develops His everlasting joy inside of us. Mature Christians are blessed with an appreciation for the gift of adoption.

SPIRITUAL BLESSING #3
The Joy of Redemption

Christ redeemed you and me. He bought us back with a ransom. He purchased us. The wages of sin is death. Death means hell. Realizing that He has purchased us is key to growing up in His everlasting joy.

Somebody had to pay for the sins that you and I committed out behind the gymnasium, on the back seat of the car, on the front seat, on the hood, in the hotel, in the cafe in

Realizing that He has purchased us is key to growing up in His everlasting joy.

the back corner in the dark. Who's going to pay for all that sin? Who's going to pay for all that liquor somebody's been drinking? Who's going to pay for all that dope somebody's been snorting up their nose? Who's going to pay for all that food somebody's been over-eating? Who's going to pay for all those cigarettes somebody's been smoking? Who's going to pay for

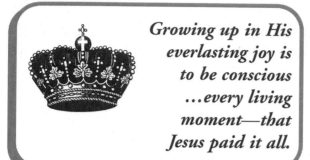

Growing up in His everlasting joy is to be conscious ...every living moment—that Jesus paid it all.

all that anger somebody's got? Who's going to pay for all that pride some people have? Somebody has got to pay!

Growing up in His everlasting joy is to be conscious— twenty-four hours a day, fifty-two weeks a year, every living moment—that Jesus paid it all. With every breath, the mature Christian (one who has grown up to the Head) is aware that he or she does not belong to self because that person has been bought for a price.

I'm reminded of the book of Hosea in which God had the prophet Hosea go buy Gomer back off the auction block after she had run out. Now, "run out" is an Alabama term. "Run out" means being "used up"—"used up" to the point of being worthless. It used to refer only to girls, but it also refers to young boys too, especially young men going off to college. They can run out, too. A young man might think he's God's gift to women, but he can run out. He can run out by the time he gets out of college. Two years out of college, nobody is going to want him. His own mama will hardly want him if he keeps on doing what he's doing. Gomer had run out. She used to be fine, a good-looking woman, but now she was on the auction block. Nobody wanted her. God demonstrated His love for all humanity when He sent His prophet Hosea to go and buy her off the auction block.

Some of us have been on the auction block. Our sins have put us right on the auction block, and God, in His compassionate Self, demonstrated His love for us through His Son, Jesus

Christ, by the blood that purchased us to be His own—the blood that makes us new. God bought us off the auction block when no one else wanted us. That is a spiritual blessing; another layer in growing up (maturing) in His everlasting joy.

SPIRITUAL BLESSING #4
The Joy of Wisdom

Have you ever been divinely guided on how to handle a difficult situation? Did words of strength and comfort come from your lips, yet you didn't know why? They are our blessing. Recognizing that this wisdom is a blessing and not the result of our own doing is growth in everlasting joy.

Read Ephesians 1:8. He's given us His grace with all wisdom and understanding. The New International Version states that not only have we been granted wisdom, but that He lavished it upon us. Have you ever lavished yourself in something or been lavished? That means it is extravagant, excessive—nothing is held back in the giving. Growing up in His everlasting joy means lavishing ourselves in His wisdom.

It's something to know "from whence cometh my help." When we are in Christ we know it is He who has brought us this far. When we know who has brought us this far, we claim nothing for ourselves. Growing up to the Head in His everlasting joy causes us to rest in the knowledge that all of our help comes from Him. We rely on no one else.

SPIRITUAL BLESSING #5
The Joy of Knowing

God has revealed the mystery of His will unto us. What a blessing! Mystery in the Bible is not like Alfred Hitchcock. Hitchcock created suspense. Biblical mystery means something was hidden and now is revealed in relationship to the will of God.

He's revealed to us the purpose of His church. He revealed to Greenforest Community Baptist Church a mystery that He's had with me for seventeen years for the vision of the church: build a biblical community of loving relationships whose members daily and devoutly love, follow, and model Christ. He's revealed His will to our membership relative to the purpose of the church which is to find them, bring them in, grow them up and send them out. God has revealed that He enjoys our praises.

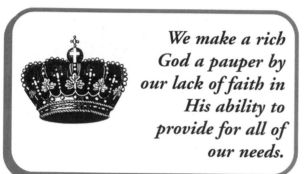

We make a rich God a pauper by our lack of faith in His ability to provide for all of our needs.

Being shrouded in ignorance, confusion and spiritual darkness is extremely frustrating. Because God loves us, He has revealed certain things to us. When we know better, we can do His will. When we do His will, the result is everlasting joy. Anyone having lived in spiritual darkness knows without a doubt that divine discernment is a spiritual blessing. It is like stumbling around in a dark room until someone finally flicks the light switch. Thank God for that light.

SPIRITUAL BLESSING #6
The Joy of Inheritance

He's given us an inheritance. We are not heirs to the estate of a pauper but to a holy and wealthy estate. Sometimes we forget that in the church as well as in our personal lives. We make a rich God a pauper by our lack of faith in His ability to provide for all of our needs. Critical to growing up in everlasting joy is realizing that everything God has is ours. His throne is ours. When we have grown up in everlasting joy, we can celebrate the fact that we are heirs to a wealthy estate.

SPIRITUAL BLESSING #7
The Joy of Being Sealed

We have a holy heritage in Him. And, guess what? In Ephesians 1:13-14 God sealed it with His Holy Spirit. He guaranteed it. God guaranteed that I would be delivered in heaven. You may get happy over a Mercedes, but I get

> *Growing up in His everlasting joy causes us to love the Giver more than the gift.*

happy over the fact that God says, "I guarantee that George McCalep has a place around the throne." No matter what model car you may get, it's going to get old. A newer, sleeker model will come along soon enough. Even if your car stays new and shiny, it may get stolen or totaled in a car accident. That's why the joy of a car or any other material thing cannot last. You can't get everlasting joy from a Benz, a BMW, a Lexus or an Infinity. Growing up in His everlasting joy causes us to love the Giver more than the gift. Growing up means we can appreciate the things He gives us yet love Him more than anything we have.

But as for my inheritance, God sealed it. It's a done deal. I can't even mess it up if I try! Now that's cause for everlasting joy. Every time I slip or "fall by the wayside," I know my inheritance is still in tact. Sometimes parents or other elders will threaten to cut someone out of their will because they messed up, but God doesn't do that because He has promised, and He keeps His Word, even when we don't.

Still, some of us have tried to mess up our inheritance. But it's a done deal. The Holy Spirit has sealed it. That's serious shouting news! I say it this way: He chose us … He redeemed us … He sealed us to the praise and glory of God.

To complete our growth toward everlasting joy, a mark has been put upon us. Have you ever gone shopping for a big ticket item like a car, a house, an appliance or furniture, only to find that the very item you wanted had a "sold" tag on it. God has tagged us, "SOLD" in big, bold print. In other words, because we believe in His Son, God has said, "That's my child." God's seal is upon us. We have been "tagged" as belonging to Him.

The Holy Spirit serves as a deposit for our guarantee that we have been purchased by Him. It may even be said that the Holy Spirit is our collateral, a deposit or guarantee that the purchase is good and secure. The collateral is worth a trillion times more than the purchase. Have you ever been pleased to get a good deal? Well, salvation is the best deal you can ever get. No gimmicks… it's guaranteed! Growing up in His everlasting joy means rejoicing over the claim He has on us.

Growing up in His everlasting joy means rejoicing over the claim He has on us.

What greater security can be provided? God's seal is upon us, claiming us as His. That claim is guaranteed by the power and presence of the Holy Spirit.

CONCLUSION

Spiritual blessings are superior to material blessings. Material blessings are temporary and fleeting, never giving fullness of His everlasting joy. Spiritual blessings are eternal. Material blessings satisfy the outer person, but spiritual blessings satisfy the inner person.

> *Spiritual blessings provide for everlasting joy, which sustains us during the most difficult times.*

There is a huge plantation that still stands in Huntsville, Alabama. A street there is named after the man who once owned the plantation. It was a great plantation with horses and with grass cut so beautifully. As a poor boy, I used to pass by there and look at the master's plantation. I remember when I got the word that the owner had committed suicide. I'll never forget that. How so, with all that plantation? When I pass by there now, the grass is overgrown, the paint is peeling off the house and it needs a new roof.

You see, spiritual blessings benefit the inner being. Spiritual blessings erase loneliness, alienation, and the lack of purpose that a person may have. Spiritual blessings give each human being a purpose. Spiritual blessings provide for everlasting joy, which sustains us during the most difficult times.

Had the plantation owner possessed His everlasting joy, he would not have taken his own life. When we grow up to the Head in His everlasting joy, we realize that our life does not belong to us. The plantation owner had all the external trappings of joy, yet joy was not in his heart. All of the things he possessed, all the beauty of his external surroundings could not impart everlasting joy—joy which sustains itself during all cir-

> *Spiritual blessings, however, do not belong to everybody. Spiritual blessings belong only to those who are in Christ.*

cumstances. If we have everlasting joy, we will value life, the worth and dignity of every individual, thereby making us a prepared vessel for Kingdom-building and local church growth.

God bestows material blessings on *everybody*. He causes the sun to shine and the rain to fall on the righteous and the unrighteous. He gives material blessings to everybody. Spiritual blessings, however, do not belong to everybody. Spiritual blessings belong only to those who are in Christ. God may give material blessings to the unrighteous. But only to the righteous, those who are in Christ, does He bestow the spiritual blessings, the most precious of gifts.

When a person is in Christ, he or she sits in heaven with Christ. How so? In God's mind, faith in Christ makes a person just like Christ. Therefore, when a person believes in Christ, God's mind sees the person in Christ. God sees the person identified with Christ seated in heaven, experiencing all the blessings of heaven in Christ with Christ. Everybody ought to want to be in Christ. Everybody ought to want to grow up in His everlasting joy.

But it takes work to grow up in the joy that never leaves. First, you must be in Christ. If you're in Christ, God takes your faith and turns it into righteousness. That righteousness will turn sorrow into joy. I'm glad to be in Christ. If you want these spiritual blessings and you're outside the ark of safety, you ought to get out of your rut, out of your mediocre life, and get back in touch with your True Love, Christ Jesus.

A lot of people want the joy He brings. But they confuse joy with happiness. The everlasting joy which results from God's out-pouring of spiritual blessings does not always mean you will be happy. It does not mean you will experience no difficulty. What it does mean is that, knowing you have received these spiritual gifts, you

A filled believer, grown up in His everlasting joy, will help produce a full house on Sunday morning.

will have within you restful peace and joy which no one can take away because they do not depend on circumstances. When we have grown up in His everlasting joy, we know that the soul's rest does not depend on our circumstances.

APPLICATION

How does growing up in His everlasting joy translate to Kingdom-building and church growth? The results of the believer growing up in His everlasting joy are evident in at least four areas.

First is in the area of being a witness or a living testimony. Believers who have grown up in His everlasting joy are contagious Christians. By their lifestyle of peace and joy, even in the midst of difficulty, they draw others to them. They become a living epistle and a living sermon. The benefit to the local church is a full house. A filled believer, growing up in His everlasting joy, will help produce a full house on Sunday morning.

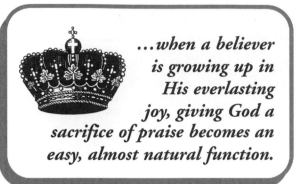

...when a believer is growing up in His everlasting joy, giving God a sacrifice of praise becomes an easy, almost natural function.

Second, a believer who has grown up to the Head in the area of everlasting joy claims victory over anger. Joy controls anger in a mature believer. Anger stifles spiritual growth. An outside observer can identify an angry person or the unresolved anger within a person. When people visit the church and they hear anger in the pastor, the Gospel is stifled. When new members join the church and view anger in the leadership, they often leave. Angry church meetings have damaged the spirit of many Christians and put a lid on many local churches. Growing up in His everlasting joy removes the lid and allows the church to grow. When a believer takes inventory of the spiritual blessings they have in Christ, it is difficult to be angry for any sustained period of time. Counting spiritual blessings helps you control your anger. If the believer wants to be an anointed blessing for the body of Christ in the place where he or she serves, that person must learn to count spiritual blessings day by day.

Third, when a believer is growing up in His everlasting joy, giving God a sacrifice of praise becomes an easy, almost natural function. The Bible tells us that praise should not be determined by our situations or circumstances. Therefore, at all times, we are to bring God a sacrifice of praise (Hebrews 13:15). However, this is easier said than done. You may be asking, "How do I praise God when life's adversities and death's shadow are upon me?" For me, it becomes easier when I understand who I am in Christ; that He chose me, redeemed me and sealed me. The believer who has grown up in everlasting joy will, at all times, bring God a sacrifice of praise. The result is that others will be drawn to Christ. "And I, if I be lifted

> *Believers who grow up in His everlasting joy will grow tall in both giving and sharing.*

up from the earth, will draw all men unto me" (John 12:32).

Fourth, the believer who has grown up in His everlasting joy will grow tall in giving. That doesn't just mean the amount. Growing tall in giving also has something to do with the spirit in which the giving is done. It is possible to be the highest giver in the church and still not have grown tall. It is possible to be on more committees and in more auxiliaries than anyone else in the church. But if the giving of time, talent and tithe is done to impress others or is done grudgingly, that person has not grown tall in giving.

In 1960, when I was coaching basketball in South Alabama, a popular cheer developed in the subculture of that small basketball community. The cheer was simply, "Grow tall!" The coach, the players on the bench and the spectators alike would cheer loudly and respectively, "Grow tall! Grow tall! Grow tall!" Obviously, tallness or height is an advantageous component of the game of basketball, but so is it in the game of life. If we are to live victoriously, we must grow tall. What a blessing to the local church as well as to the believer! Those who have grown up in the everlasting joy of giving find that giving and serving are a privilege and a joy, not a duty or chore.

We will never be fully grown up in Him until we put Ephesians 4:28 into practice: "… But rather let him labour, working with his hands the thing which is good, that he may have to give to him that needeth." Can you imagine a local church whose believers practice what God has said to do in Ephesians 4:28? The house will not only be full, but the will of God will also be done.

Growing tall in giving does not include just giving money. It includes all manner of giving, especially giving and sharing the love of Christ. Paul's closing statement to the church at Ephesus (Ephesians 6:21-24), admonishes the church to give to each other personal encouragement, peace and God's love and grace.

Believers who grow up in His everlasting joy will grow tall in both giving and sharing. Giving and sharing are key components to church growth. The believer who grows up to the Head in His everlasting joy will eventually lead the local body of believers to grow in number.

FOR STUDY AND REVIEW

Chapter One
Growing Up to the Head in His Everlasting Joy

1. This book is based on the study of the Book of _____ .

2. The ability to praise God in all circumstances does not come to us automatically. Our human nature causes us not to praise God at every turn of life. At what turns of your life have you failed to praise God?

3. A great part of growing up to the Head involves conforming our nature to that of the Head. Name some specific ways in which your old nature has conformed to the Head.

4. In order for the church to grow up to the Head in His everlasting joy, the church must grow "out" of (check one):
   _____ excessive Bible study
   _____ materialism
   _____ proportion

5. Growing up to the Head in His everlasting joy means thinking more about the _____ _____ of God.

6. List the seven spiritual blessings:

   1. _____

   2. _____

   3. _____

   4. _____

   5. _____

   6. _____

   7. _____

7. How can an entire church body grow up in everlasting joy?

8. What are the symptoms of a church that is lacking His everlasting joy?

Growing Up in His Word

1. Read the entire Book of Ephesians (preferably from a contemporary translation). Match each chapter with its primary theme.

    _____ Unity in the Body

    _____ Made alive in Christ

    _____ Spiritual blessings

    _____ The armor of God

    _____ Children of the light

    _____ Servant of the Gospel

2. Focus your attention on Ephesians 1:15-23. What are the three areas Paul prayed God would reveal, or give enlightenment, to those at the church of Ephesus?

    1. _____

    2. _____

    3. _____

Growing Up Together

1. What does it mean to be "in Christ" and how does it relate to having His everlasting joy?

Growing Up to the Head!

1. Identify seven things in your life that bring you "happiness."

   1. _____

   2. _____

   3. _____

   4. _____

   5. _____

   6. _____

   7. _____

2. Compare those seven things with the seven spiritual blessings which bring His everlasting joy. Answer the following questions, which will assist you in growing up to the Head in His everlasting joy.

   a. How did I obtain the things that give me "happiness" ... the things that give me "joy"?

   b. Can the absence of the things which give me "happiness" affect my relationship with God? What about absence of the things that give me "joy"?

   c. Based on the answers to (a) and (b) above, where should your attention be focused? Where is your attention focused?

GROWING UP TO THE HEAD

In His Grace

When our youngest son felt he had grown up, he decided he wanted to move out and be his own man. He felt the rules of our house were too confining.

For by grace are ye saved through faith; and that not of yourselves: it is the gift of God.   *Ephesians 2:8*

After he had sufficient time to experience what it really meant to be "on his own"—including paying all the bills—he was ready to move back home. He found that the privilege of not having to worry about certain things was worth whatever personal sacrifices he had to make. My son had to mature enough to realize that it was a blessing to live under the comfort and protection of his parents' house.

God's grace is a privilege we have because God loves us. Sometimes we have to grow up enough to understand that there are some things we cannot control or change and that those things are covered by grace. But there are times when we don't want to make any personal sacrifices. For God's people, that sacrifice usually involves giving up control of our lives. It involves acknowledging who is Supreme. Growing up in His grace means letting God rule our hearts and minds.

We have all played the role of prodigal child at some point in our lives. Every person has thought, "I can do it better my way." Most, if not all of us, have even played the role of prodigal child with our heavenly Father a few times. We may think, "I'm just going to do this…"—having no regard for the consequences. When we choose to go our own way and rebel against God, we are proud and self-confident. Later, as we find the need to return to

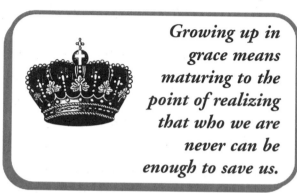

Growing up in grace means maturing to the point of realizing that who we are never can be enough to save us.

Him, with an empty, humble and contrite heart, God stands ready to receive us. Growing up in grace means maturing to the point of realizing that who we are can never be enough to save us. It means understanding that God is perfect and we are always at His mercy. Further, it means taking comfort in His mercy.

Ephesians 2:8 tells us that we are not saved by our own deeds—salvation is God's gift. No one should boast, Paul says, about what he or she has done. Paul is saying, "Take this as a gift and don't be foolish enough to think that you earned it. In fact, don't even try to think that you can earn the gift of salvation!" Or, in the vernacular of Generation X, "Don't even go there!"

GROWING UP TO DEPENDENCY

Our Western cultural values encourage us to grow up to be independent. As we grow from childhood to adolescence to adulthood, we are supposed to progressively strive for greater independence. The meaning of growing up in His grace is nearly the exact opposite of growing up in the world. As we grow up in grace, we learn to become more *dependent* upon God, *not independent.* The more we mature as Christians, the greater our dependency upon Him should be. In fact, we should strive to mature spiritually to the point that we become like children, just as Jesus told us in Matthew18:3: "Except ye be converted, and become as little children, ye shall not enter into the kingdom of heaven." Jesus was teaching this because He knew that we would have to become like children to grow up spiritually.

There is a story that has often been told about a father and his five-year-old daughter who went out sailing one day. The boat capsized, and the two found themselves stranded in the middle of nowhere. The father decided to attempt to swim back to shore. Before he left his young daughter, he asked her, "Do you remember when Daddy taught you how to float?" She replied, "Yes, Daddy, I remember." Her father instructed her to float there on the water until he returned for her.

The man was found by the Coast Guard. He told them his little girl was still out there. They searched the spot where the boat had sunk, to no avail. The Coast Guardsmen presumed her to be dead. They tried to console the father. He convinced them to go out looking for her once more.

This time they did find her. Not only was she alive, but she was singing a song! They asked her how she was able to sing even though she was stranded? She replied, "Well, my Daddy told me he would come back and get me. My Daddy always keeps his promises."

It takes maturity for a Christian to have as much faith in our Heavenly Father as that five-year-old girl had in her daddy. We have to grow up in His grace to have the faith of a child! Jesus said become like little children. Think about a child that you know. If that child wants a new doll or a bike or a video game, he or she does not generally set about trying to earn it. Of course, children may flatter you and hint to you. But they do not set about trying to *work* to *earn* the thing they desire. They ask for what they want and then go about being who they are—children. That's what God wants from us. We need His grace. We can ask for it and then go about the business of being who we are—children of God.

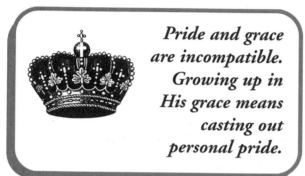

Pride and grace are incompatible. Growing up in His grace means casting out personal pride.

Acts 20:35 tells us that Jesus said, "It is more blessed to give than to receive." It is blessed to give, but for many of us, it is more difficult to receive. If I receive something from you, that implies that I am indebted to you. Some of us have a hard time with indebtedness. We pride ourselves on not owing anything to anyone. That word pride is important. Pride and grace are incompatible. Growing up in His grace means casting out personal pride.

Paul warns us in Ephesians 2:9 not to boast. The main reason Paul says this is because none of us has anything to boast about. For example, suppose you decide to test this out by taking your list of works to God, just to show how good and helpful you have been to Him. Without knowing you, I can guarantee that God can return to you a list of things you haven't done that is at least twice as long as the list of things you have done! Our righteousness is nothing. Isaiah says our righteousness is like that of filthy rags before God (Isaiah 64:6). In other words, we are like a pus-laden bandage before God. Do you have any use for a bandage filled with pus? Well, that's about how much use God has for our human righteousness. It has no value except to be discarded. We've got to discard notions of our own righteousness and stand before God covered by the blood of Jesus alone.

If you need further proof, consider the story of the Rich Young Ruler who asked Jesus, "What good thing must I do to inherit eternal life?" Jesus quickly replied that there is only One who is good. Then Jesus told the young Jewish man to obey the commandments. Not satisfied and still full of himself, the man, I'll call him Mr. Rich, told Jesus that he was already doing those things. Then, blam! Jesus hit Mr. Rich where it hurt. Jesus hit his weakness. Jesus hit the spot from which young Mr. Rich could not recover.

Up until that point, Mr. Rich thought he was earning his own way. After all, he was wealthy and faithful to the Law. According to Jewish understanding, that meant he was all right with God. But Jesus deflated Mr. Rich when He told him to sell everything he had, give it to the poor, and then follow Him. That was just too much. That was the point where grace needed to step in. The rich young man's weakness was exposed. He was unable to part with all that he had. Mr. Rich needed grace to pick up the slack and save him. Jesus told His disciples that it is impossible for any person to save himself or herself. Growing up in His grace means letting God do what only He can.

If you have a problem with being indebted to God, you will have a difficult time receiving His grace. If you don't want to be indebted to God, you don't want to grow up in His grace. Grace will always be His gift to us and our debt to Him. We will always owe God because we can never repay Him for all He has done, is doing and will continue to do. Wherever we are, whatever we do, it is all due to the grace of God. A missionary and a low-life street drug pusher are the same. My life before God is no different than that of a man condemned to

Growing up in His grace allows us to accept the fact that all that we are is due to His grace.

die in the electric chair. The only difference is that before my death sentence could be executed, Jesus issued me a reprieve by sitting in the chair and taking the punishment for me.

Jesus took the punishment because He knew that George McCalep was not able. Growing up in His grace allows us to accept the fact that all that we are is due to His grace. Jesus took your punishment and mine because He knew we were not able to take it.

Sometimes we Christians, like the rich, young ruler, can get full of ourselves. We can become really pleased with the way in which we are living for Jesus. We praise ourselves for paying our full tithe, or even above the tithe. The fact that we have chaired a major church committee effectively is cause for self-congratulation. Our children are doing well … a reflection, we think, of our good parenting and role modeling. We may have even been blessed with a little money in the bank, a decent job, a nice car and good health. That's how it happens: the more we are blessed with grace, the more we may begin to lose sight of where the blessings and abilities come from. We may even begin to think that we deserve all of

When we have grown up in His grace, we do not take His blessings for granted.

these good things because of our faithfulness. This may have happened to you at some period in your life. When we have grown up in His grace, we do not take His blessings for granted.

But what happens when the bottom falls out of your well-doing? What about when you find you've messed up in a big way? If you are honest about your sinful state, you will recognize and acknowledge when you have really messed up. You can't blame it on your wife or husband, not on your kids, not on your boss, or on the preacher. It was nobody's fault but your own. Sooner or later, you come to the realization that there is some area of your life where you just can't do any better on your own. That thing you thought you'd never do again knocks you to your knees before you know what hit you. That old bad temper; that old jealousy; that old envy; that old roaming eye; that old gossiping, angry, unforgiving heart...the weakness you thought was long gone has taken up residence in your heart once again. That old sin has returned to your heart and has become as fresh and new as the first time. That's when it's time to confess your sins and call on grace. That's when it's time to ask for what you don't deserve, haven't earned, and can't repay. But that is also the time when God can begin to work in you because you've taken the burden off yourself and put it where it belongs.

UNMERITED FAVOR

Growing up in His grace begins with realizing how unworthy we are to receive it. As long as we think we've earned some grace, we've got some growing up to do. Sometimes it's hard to make it "click" inside of us that grace is something we cannot earn. Grace is most often defined as "unmerited favor." That means we don't deserve it. That means we can't earn it. That means we should not even try to earn it.

Growing up in His grace helps us to understand that every breath we take is in His hands.

I recall a story a man told about his epiphany concerning the nature of grace. He is a large, well-built man, standing over six feet tall. One day he was walking down the street eating a muffin. A small piece of it got lodged in his windpipe, and he nearly choked to death. Someone came to his aid, but he realized it was grace that saved him. Until that time, he thought himself to be formidable against life's elements, fearing nothing. When he realized that a tiny crumb of cake could bring him to death's door, he understood the role of grace, even in the life of a physically well-built man like himself. Growing up in His grace helps us to understand that every breath we take is in His hands.

In many governmental agencies, people were hired, promoted or paid on what was known as a merit system. That meant you earned your way up—either up the chain of command or up the economic ladder. It was often a breeding ground for corrupt practices. People were earning merits based on conditions other than job performance. That is probably what would happen if God had a merit system. Can you imagine how corrupt we would try to make it? We would probably go behind one another's backs, trying to kick someone out of favor with God so that we could move ourselves in. When we grow up in His grace, we take comfort in the fact that gaining His favor is not like gaining human favor.

That's what happened to Daniel. The other high-ranking Babylonian officials were upset because Daniel had favor with the king. They thought that by removing Daniel, they would place themselves in a better position to earn favor with King Darius. Even in that circumstance, Daniel was

No amount of goodness can steer God's favor toward you.

spared from the lions' den because of God's grace. God cannot be tricked or fooled. That is why it is best for us to come before Him being straightforward and honest about our shortcomings and inadequacies. We should relax and rejoice over the fact that God loves us so much that He wants to give us a priceless gift. Unmerited favor means that we accept God's gift and leave it alone.

What does it mean to have God's favor? It means having something that no amount of money can buy. Daniel was a good man, but even he did not earn God's favor. No amount of goodness can steer God's favor toward you. Having God's favor does not mean the same as having the favor of men and women.

In her book *If Not for the Grace of God* (Harrison House, 1995), Joyce Meyer addresses the difference between human favor and divine favor. She concludes that human favor can be earned, but God's favor is a gift.

Think about it, if you work at it long enough (and hard enough), you can earn the favor of most human beings. Men have often tried to win the favor of women by having a fancy car or by telling them flattering words. Some women have used their appearance to win the favor of men; and others have tried to impress men with culinary skills. Human favor can be predicted according to how we treat people. It involves compli-

Growing up in His grace releases us from trying to earn His favor.

mentary words, encouragement, caring, nurturing and, sometimes, just having the right image.

We scramble about trying to figure out ways to earn God's favor, but we cannot. It only produces frustration. The frustration sets in as we try to do the impossible ... earn favor or merit from God. It just cannot be done. What we can do, however, is sow seeds for a harvest of godly favor. If we treat others right, giving them respect and dignity, we have fertile ground for building solid, godly relationships. But plowing fertile ground should not be done with the intention of simply awaiting God's favor. That is simply another merit system. God wants us to live our lives with freedom and liberty in the absence of legalism. Growing up in His grace releases us from trying to earn His favor.

Our Creator wants to do many things for us, but we block Him. We block Him by trying to be worthy. We block Him by being too proud to ask. We block Him by waiting until we feel we have a "right" to come before Him. Growing up in His

Growing up in His grace means knowing that we never earn what He has to give.

grace means knowing that we never earn what He has to give. Have you ever heard someone say, "I'm going to get myself straight and then I'm going to come back to church"? A person who thinks this way will never make it back to the church. No one is capable of getting or staying on the right track without the help of the Almighty. Growing up in His grace means relying on God's mercy and lovingkindness to sustain us because we can do no better for ourselves.

THE POWER OF SURRENDER

Paul says he asked the Lord three times to remove his thorn (2 Corinthians 12:8). Each time the Lord said no. When Paul understood that God's sufficiency covered his infirmities, he then surrendered. Surrender is usually associated with loss or weakness. But standing before God, surrender is the most powerful act a Christian can take. When we surrender, we acknowledge that we cannot do what only God can. Growing up in grace means rejoicing in the ability to surrender. It means giving up control to God.

In the 11th Chapter of Matthew, Jesus says, "Come unto me all ye that labour and are heavy laden, and I will give you rest. Take my yoke upon you, and learn of me; for I am meek and lowly in heart: and ye shall find rest unto your souls." Have you ever had a really difficult job to do all by yourself? Have you ever had someone offer to take a burden from you, such as a financial burden or a work load that was just too much for one person to accomplish? That's what Jesus is trying to do for each of us. He keeps trying to take the burden and lighten our load, but we won't let Him. We insist on carrying that backbreaking dead weight of sin.

Growing up in His grace means letting go of the weight we are carrying. Our Lord is standing at the door waiting for us to give Him the weight we are carrying. "Let Me have it," He says. "Let Me handle it. You just go over there and rest." Is that an offer not to be refused? If you have refused His offer, you need

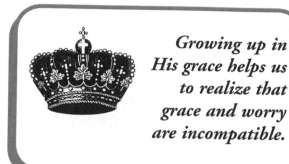

Growing up in His grace helps us to realize that grace and worry are incompatible.

to take Him up on it now. You need to give that heavy load to Jesus now; He actually wants it.

It is amazing to me how we sing, preach and praise God's ability to provide, deliver, save or whatever. But when it comes to enacting our faith in God's ability, we act as though there is no God. We can easily tell someone else to have faith. We can speak quite eloquently on the abstract notion of faith in God's ability. But when our personal faith is called to the test, we often fall short. Growing up in grace is understanding that we will fall short and that Jesus Christ picks us up when we can go no further. Once we let it go, we are free.

The journey of a Christian has sometimes been compared to the race of a long distance runner. What happens if you stumble and fall along the way? What happens if you get a cramp in your leg? What happens when you need to stop to get something to eat or drink? Who ministers to you? Who cares for you in your woundedness so that you can get back up and continue the race? Who will even pick you up and carry you across the finish line if you can't make it alone? Only Jesus will do that for you and me. Only He is able to do that for us.

Growing up in His grace means knowing when to surrender. It means knowing when things are for God alone to handle, and then leaving them alone for Him to do just that. Growing up in His grace helps us to realize that grace and worry are incompatible. Grace is freedom—grace is peace. How can we experience God's peace or God's freedom if we are in a constant state of worry? The things we really worry about are the things we cannot change. If we cannot change them, then we must trust the grace of our Lord to cover that situation like a warm blanket

Growing up in His grace closes our ears to Satan's messages of shame, guilt, worry and doubt.

covers and protects us when we are cold. If we cannot change them, we must surrender them to grace.

The things we really worry about are generally in the past or have not yet happened. Neither the past nor the future can be altered or fixed by human effort. God does not change our past, but His grace turns the stumbling blocks of our past into stepping stones. A murderer cannot bring back the life of the one he killed, but God's grace can take what is left of the murderer's life, turn it around and use it for good. An adulteress cannot change her past deed, but God can renew her and give her strength, perhaps to help another from falling into the same trap. Satan tries to keep us in remembrance of our past. He tries to keep us in a state of shame, guilt, worry and doubt. The devil tries to keep us in bondage when God's grace has made us free. Growing up in His grace closes our ears to Satan's negative, discouraging messages.

Psalm 103:12 tells us, "As far as the east is from the west, so far hath he removed our transgressions from us." Now, as far as I know, the east and the west never come together, they just get further apart. That's how far God's grace removes our past sins from our present and future. There is a story about a little girl who told a priest that she had been speaking with Jesus. The old priest did not believe her, but the child persisted. Finally the priest said, "Okay, the next time you talk to Him, ask Him to tell you what my last sin was." The little girl came back to the priest and said, "I spoke to Jesus and asked Him about your last sin." Curious, the old priest responded, "Really? And what did He tell you?" The child replied, "He said He forgot."

When we surrender to Him, all is forgiven and forgotten. It is Satan who tries to imprison us once again with guilt and shame after Christ has set us free. It is Satan who wants us to think we are not worthy to serve our Lord because of our past. It is also Satan who wants to cripple us with fear about the future. When we are paralyzed with fear, God cannot use us. Fear

Growing up to the Head in His grace allows us to surrender to Him.

paralyzes; surrender releases. If you find yourself stuck, unable to move or grow to do anything for Christ, surrender! Just give it up! His arms are outstretched, just waiting to receive all your burdens. When we are consumed with thoughts of fear and worry, we have no time to focus on godly things: we have no energy to devote to the Kingdom; we have no faith to see God has a better plan for our future. Growing up to the Head in His grace allows us to surrender to Him.

Fear and worry can make us think that God is as powerless as we are. It can cause us to forget His power. We forget His many names:

Jehovah Jireh — the One who provides
Jehovah Nissi — the Victor, our Banner, our Standard
Jehovah Rohi — our Shepherd who causes us not to want for any good thing

El-Elyon	— the Most High God
El-Shaddai	— God Almighty of blessings
Elohim	— Creator of heaven and earth
Yahweh	— I Am

When God explained Himself to Moses, He simply said, "My name is I AM." It is interesting that God gave no noun to limit Himself. He did not say simply, "I am Love" or "I am Peace" or "I am Providence." By calling Himself "I AM," God opened the way for us to understand Him as all we need Him to be. It has been said over and over in many churches, "He's a Mother for the motherless … He's a Father for the fatherless … He's Shelter in a storm … He's Light in darkness … He's a Friend to the friendless." Growing up in His grace opens our hearts to knowing that God is everything we need.

God described Himself as a verb, not a noun. A noun is self-containing. A verb is action. God becomes all we need Him to be when we need Him to be it. God is a verb, taking action in every area of our lives. We can surrender to the God of action because He is moving, always taking care of His children.

> *Growing up in grace involves understanding the process. God has given us a great inheritance.*

THREE STAGES OF GROWING

Growing up in grace involves understanding the process. God has given us a great inheritance. Growing up to the Head in grace involves three stages. The first stage can be found in Ephesians 2:1-3: "And you hath he quickened, who were dead in trespasses and sins; Wherein in time past ye walked according to the course of

Growing up to the Head in His grace helps us to understand the power of the flesh.

this world, according to the prince of the power of the air, the spirit that now worketh in the children of disobedience: Among whom also we all had our conversation in times past in the lusts of our flesh, fulfilling the desires of the flesh and of the mind; and were by nature the children of wrath, even as others."

The first stage is when we are "in the flesh." That is the time when we live for what pleases us. Nothing is more important than going after what we desire. Some people live their entire life in that mode. They never consider what is beyond the works of the flesh. Circumstances may sometimes force some people into that mode. For instance, a man or woman who is homeless is first concerned for survival—food, drink, shelter for the night. That's why it is nearly futile to speak with a hungry or destitute person about the Gospel until we have gotten that person's attention by ministering to his or her immediate needs. That is simply our human nature.

Growing up to the Head in His grace helps us to understand the power of the flesh. Christians need to remember the power of the flesh when we witness. Not that we are to con-

In order to establish a relationship with the unsaved, we need to find a point of entry.

done the lifestyle of the unsaved, but we need a point of reference to begin establishing a relationship. We need to especially be sensitive to those who are relational people. Some people are less likely to read through the "Plan of Salvation" and say, "Aha! I want Jesus to come into my heart." In order to establish a relationship with the unsaved, we need to find a point of entry. The point of reference that opens a space for dialogue varies with each person. For some, it is basic physical needs: food, clothing, employment, and so forth. Growing up in His grace gives us compassion for those who are still hurting because we remember how far He has brought us.

Pain, for instance, is a powerful prison cell. A person who is trapped in a painful lifestyle can't get out to see God's love and His desire for all humankind to be saved. Poor marital or family relationships, or being trapped in a lifestyle of excesses (spending, drugs, sex, food, gambling alcohol) is prison. A sinner caught in a trap of the flesh desperately needs to know about God's grace. A believer caught in a fleshly trap cannot possibly

A believer caught in a fleshly trap cannot possibly grow up to the Head in grace.

grow up to the Head in grace. Someone has to help point to the Way, knowing that every believer has been there at some point. Eventually, all of humankind comes to God at this point, having lived in darkness, living only for earthly pleasures.

The second stage is when God stepped in. He had to help us, for we could not help ourselves. Verses 4-7 in the 2nd Chapter of Ephesians read: "But God, who is rich in mercy, for his great love wherewith he loved us, Even when we were dead in sins, hath quickened us together with Christ (by grace ye are saved). And hath raised us up together, and made us sit together in heavenly places in Christ Jesus: That in the ages to come he might show the exceeding riches of his grace in his kindness toward us through Christ Jesus."

Growing up in His grace means understanding that we cannot save ourselves.

Every believer is a walking, breathing living example of God's grace. Growing up in His grace means understanding that we are a product of grace. Out of God's love and mercy, He looked upon us, knowing we could not help ourselves. Therefore, He sent His Son Jesus and resurrected Him from the grave to give us victory over sin and death. Have you ever seen a small child trying to do something that is beyond his ability to do? If you watch him for a while, you realize the futility of his efforts. The child himself may even know it but will still try to do the task because he knows something needs to be done. That's about the time you step in to lend a hand—a stronger, more capable hand. You then help the child complete the task he could never do on his own.

That's the way God looked upon us. We could never save ourselves. Growing up in His grace means understanding that we cannot save ourselves. We were desperately trying to follow the Law, futile as our efforts were. It was impossible for us to perfect it. God watched our failing efforts with mercy and love. He had to send Jesus to us because it was obvious we couldn't do any better. What a relief to know we don't have to do it! Even though it is impossible for us, we still may have tried doing it our way. Until God stepped in, humanity was simply sinking deeper and deeper. When we have grown up in His grace, we rejoice in the fact that He is our Rescuer.

When we have grown up in His grace, we rejoice in the fact that He is our Rescuer.

Many parents, especially in this age of "easy credit," have experienced having to help an adult child get out of debt. You may have even experienced it yourself. For instance, you may have an adult daughter who got caught in the credit trap. The "easy" credit terms seemed so appealing to her. In this country, once you are approved for one credit card, the floodgates open. Out of nowhere come offers for additional credit cards. What started out for that young woman as "easy" has now become a massive debt, one that she can never repay on her income. She realizes she is in over her head and comes to you, head bowed and humble, to confess that she is in a situation that is greater than she can handle. Even though the indebtedness is of her own doing, as a loving parent you step in and pay off her debts. You know that she is not and will never be able to repay you or the credit companies. Out of her love and gratitude, your daughter may give you money at times because she knows what you have done for her. But the actual debt itself cannot be repaid. Even if she spent her entire lifetime trying to pay you back, she never could. Even if she paid you back the entire dollar amount, with interest, she can never repay you for what you did for her at that moment in time. If you, the loving parent, had not stepped in, she would have spent the rest of her life trapped in a cycle of indebtedness.

God, the Father, is our Loving Parent. When we were sinking deep in sin, indebted far beyond what we could ever pay, God stepped in and paid our debt in full with the blood of Jesus Christ. He knew we couldn't help it. He knew we needed help. Growing up in His grace means realizing He has

Growing up in His grace means realizing He has paid a debt we can never repay.

paid a debt we can never repay. And try as we might to repay Him, and give honor and praise to Him out of love and gratitude for what He has done, we can never repay the debt. God lifted us out of sin when we were deep in it. That is what sin does. It attracts you by making you think it is easy. Then once you are trapped, you are helpless if you don't know Jesus. A sinner is sinking as deeply as the daughter in debt. But, like the daughter, all the sinner has to do is come to the Loving Parent and confess the indebtedness. There are sinners out there right now trying to free themselves from the grip of a debt to the world out of which they cannot pull themselves. The Loving Father is rich and ready to repay the debt for them if they ask. He is ready to tell the world that humanity's debt for sin is "paid in full." Growing up in grace means we do not wear ourselves out trying to repay an impossible debt.

Stage three is knowing that the debt has been paid for us by Jesus Christ as our gift from the Loving Father. Ephesians 2:8-10 helps us understand how this happened: "For by grace are ye saved through faith; and that not of yourselves: it is the gift of God: Not of works, lest any man should boast. For we are his workmanship, created in Christ Jesus unto good

> *When we have grown up in His grace, we know we have done nothing to brag about.*

works, which God hath before ordained that we should walk in them."

Paul is reminding us there is no room to brag on ourselves. When we have grown up in His grace, we know we have done nothing to brag about. Think about the daughter who was raised out of debt by her loving parents. Could she boast to anyone about what she did for herself to change her condition? Of course not. She may share her story with her friends in a similar condition. She may tell them to go to their loving parents who stand ready to help. She may tell the story of "how I got over," but there is no room in that story for self-aggrandizement. If we try to boast about how good we are, we look as foolish as that daughter bragging about how she got herself out of debt.

Growing up in grace is knowing that our present state and God's plan of salvation is His gift to us. It is a gift rooted in love. We cheapen His gift when we try to take

> *We cheapen His gift when we try to take credit for any of it ourselves.*

credit for any of it ourselves. How can anyone give you a gift which you helped to pay for? Can a husband claim his wife gave him a new suit as a gift if he had to help pay for it? Can a child claim a new bicycle as a gift from her parents if she helped pay for it herself? That would be contrary to the definition of a gift. In this age of gimmick advertising, we often see the words "free gift" used; but people are generally suspicious that nothing is free. And in fact, nothing really is. It has been said that some people prefer the word "complimentary" rather than "free" because everything costs something. Their rationale is that even if the recipient did not pay the price, someone did.

Even some of our televangelists have begun to misuse the word gift. Often, you will see them offering a book or a tape as a "gift" when you send a love offering. In this age, the message implies that if you don't send the love offering, you don't receive the gift. Is it any wonder there is so much distrust concerning the gift of salvation? Should those who are unsaved be suspicious about the offer of salvation, for which nothing need be paid?

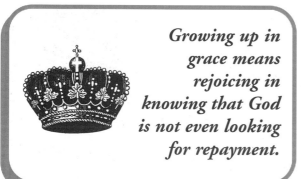

Growing up in grace means rejoicing in knowing that God is not even looking for repayment.

Jesus paid the price for our salvation, but that price was paid by the grace of God. It is not an "advertising" gift. It is not a "gimmick" gift. It is not a gift that is given because it is worn or outdated. There is no trick or gimmick to God's grace. Growing up to the Head in His grace is knowing that the gift of salvation was bought at a premium, with Jesus' blood. It also means knowing and even rejoicing in the fact that we have a priceless gift which we will never be able to repay Him. Furthermore, it means rejoicing in knowing that God is not even looking for repayment. Finally, growing up in grace means inner peace and security because we have the assurance of salvation.

APPLICATION

How does growing up in His grace apply to the growth of one church? That makes me wonder: How many persons with great potential has the Church had an opportunity to claim for Jesus yet didn't because of their unsavory past? Some of the most faithful and dedicated church workers are often those who have come out of the most worldly lifestyles. But such people will only come to the church if the church is open to receiving them. Churches with members who are long on judgement and short on acceptance have not grown up to the Head in His grace. How many would-be Christians has the church lost because it overlooked persons who were trapped in the garbage heap of life? How many potential soldiers has the army of the Lord lost because our churches have not grown up to the Head in His grace? How many of our churches are stagnant or haven't had a new member come in the church in twenty years because the members are not growing in up grace? If the members are immature concerning their knowledge and experience with grace, then the church body will be no better. An unforgiving, closed-spirited person has to find a church that will allow him or her to nurture and maintain an unforgiving spirit.

> *How many potential soldiers has the army of the Lord lost because our churches have not grown up to the Head in grace?*

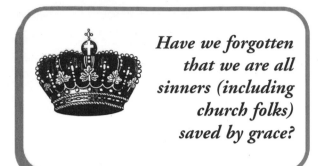

Have we forgotten that we are all sinners (including church folks) saved by grace?

On the contrary, a person who is growing in His grace would have a difficult time being a part of a church that is cold, unforgiving and full of condemnation. Grace and condemnation are incompatible. Paul says in Romans 8:1, "There is therefore now no condemnation to them which are in Christ Jesus, who walk not after the flesh, but after the Spirit." How, then, can we condemn fellow Christians or those who seek to escape eternal condemnation? How can the church sit in judgement of another?

In Romans 10:13, Paul says, "For whosoever shall call upon the name of the Lord shall be saved." That means if a murderer calls on the name of the Lord, he shall be saved. But a church which is immature in grace will not make room for even a murderer who has been saved by grace through faith. A church that has not grown up in grace cannot understand that the church is simply a hospital for the spiritually sick. In a hospital for the physically sick, there are varying degrees of illness. The same is true for the church. Believers who are growing up in grace know better than to put themselves above others, no matter what others have done in the past.

Something in our insecure human nature wants some of us to feel as though we are morally or spiritually superior to some others. Those of us who feel this way cause people outside the church to say, "When I get myself right, I'm coming (back) to church." What has the Christian church done to give those who are outside the church the impression that they must "get right" in order to come among us? Have we forgotten that we are all sinners (including church folks) saved by grace? That same spirit of immaturity concerning grace has caused many others to condemn the church, casting it aside as irrelevant. Many of these people know and have seen many "good church folk" out in the world demonstrating everything but a saving knowledge of Jesus Christ. Yet, the same folk would pass judgement on others to determine who is worthy to come to church and who is not.

An older seminary professor told his class a story about two men who were members of the "premier" church in their city. One man, an alcoholic, owned a dry cleaning business and cleaned the church's choir and minister's robes at no charge to them. He was ashamed of his condition and would not come to the church, but he offered what he felt he had—dry cleaning at no charge. Of his service to the church he said, "No, I can't come, but I want to do this."

> *When we grow up in His grace, we are more concerned about another's salvation than our own reputation.*

The other man, the professor said, attended church regularly and was active as a deacon. By contrast, the other man also owned a business which provided goods to the church. This man did not provide his company's goods to the church for free, though. In fact, he charged them a higher price than he charged other customers! He rationalized his position thusly: "Well, the church can afford to pay a little extra."

After telling the story, the professor asked his students, "Which man exhibited more of a spirit of Christianity." The class determined that the alcoholic who felt unworthy to be in the Lord's house had demonstrated a greater spirit of Christianity than did the deacon who was an active member of the church. What made the deacon feel more worthy to be in God's house than the alcoholic? Perhaps both men could have used a lesson on grace. The alcoholic man needed grace to uplift him and the deacon needed to come to an awareness of his own weakness. When we have grown up in grace, we are aware of our own weaknesses.

> *Growing up to the Head in grace results in honest and transparent lives. People looking for a church home respond to openness and honesty.*

Jesus was often criticized for those with whom He associated because they were not Judaism's finest. Today, many churches want only their town's finest to come into the church. They want to criticize whoever comes in and vote on who can come in. They want to somehow place a dividing wall between themselves and the sinner seeking salvation or wholeness. Many people have been killed spiritually because their church was short of grace. When we grow up in His grace, we are more concerned about another's salvation than our own reputation.

A friend of mine (who is also a pastor) was once offered a prominent position with an agency in his denomination. My friend refused to apply for the position. He explained to the man who had encouraged him to apply, "No, I would not qualify for that job because I am divorced and you don't hire divorced people. But even if you all can't forgive me for that, I know that God has." In other words, Christians are holding things against people and keeping them out of the body of Christ even though God has already forgiven them. Why do we feel so important and worthy? Growing up to the Head in His grace opens our eyes to the fact that grace is in His hands, not ours. By withholding the message of grace, however, some churches have kept people in shame and guilt. These churches have unknowingly encouraged people to live closed, closeted lives. Such churches seem to reward living a lie and condemn confession of the soul.

Growing up in His grace means learning to shout hallelujah every time somebody wants to make a step out of darkness …

We live in the midst of a lost and hurting world. This hurting world is looking for somewhere to take its hurts. Can they bring them to your church? Has your church grown up to the Head so that it is willing to accept the same criticism that Jesus did for having, the "wrong" type of people around him? It takes strong spiritual maturity to be able to cast aside what others think and draw from life's garbage heap. Growing up to the Head in grace results in honest and transparent lives.

People looking for a church home respond to openness and honesty—the ability to say, "I love Jesus, but I still have problems … I love the Lord, but I'm having a little trouble paying my bills right now … I love Jesus, but my

A lot of church growth comes from the garbage heap.

Growing up in grace means knowing that all of us were in that garbage heap of life at one time.

spouse and I are having some problems ... I believe in His power, but I'm tired a lot because I'm caring for my mother who is dying ... I know things will get better, but I lost my job last week ..." This is what people are looking for. It seems to me that men, particularly, are attracted to churches where the members are honest and living transparent lives. Many men complain about the hypocrisy of preachers and of the church. They think the pastor is either going with the ladies in the church or that he's taking all the money from the church.

The church that has grown up to the Head in grace has a soft sponge to accompany the bucket of healing waters that come from Jesus Christ and the sweet-smelling soap of salvation for those who wish to come out of life's garbage heap. Only Jesus has the cleansing power, but the church can provide the soft sponge to aid in the cleansing process. When a church is full of members who are growing up in grace, they are not afraid of life's garbage heap. Growing up in His grace means learning to shout hallelujah every time somebody wants to make a step out of darkness ... every time somebody wants to confess a bad habit so they can march toward freedom ... every time somebody wants to unload their burden at the altar of the Lord.

A lot of church growth comes from the garbage heap. For church growth to occur, the people already in the church must be willing to go back to the heap and get some folk out. A church that is waiting only for the sweet-smelling folk will be waiting a long time for growth. Growing up in grace means knowing that all of us were in that garbage heap of life, at one time. Some are simply a little deeper down in the heap's pile.

People who are living in life's garbage heap are everywhere. Sometimes, while waiting for a traffic light to change, I observe a downtrodden pedestrian crossing the street, choking the neck of a liquor bottle, thinly disguised in a brown paper bag. Have you seen him, or one like him, while you are sitting in traffic? He seems to appear in every town and city. Every time I see him, I say, "If not for the grace of God, there go I." Growing up to the Head in grace is learning to say, "If not for the grace of God, there go I."

FOR STUDY AND REVIEW

Chapter Two
Growing Up to the Head in His Grace

1. What is the definition of grace? Identify a time in your life when you were blessed with God's grace.

2. Growing up in His grace means letting God rule our _____ and _____ .

3. In order for a church to grow up in His grace, the body must be totally dependent on God and interdependent on each other. (check one) True ___ or False ___ .

4. From which of life's garbage heaps did God pull you? How did it help you to understand grace?

5. Pride and _____ are incompatible! We must discard all notions of our own _____.

6. What are the three stages of growing?
   a. _____
   b. _____
   c. _____

7. A church that has not grown up in grace cannot understand that the church is simply a hospital for the _____ _____.

Growing Up in His Word

1. Re-read the Book of Ephesians. Focus your attention on Chapter 2:1-20. Explain what it means to be made "alive in Christ" as it relates to salvation and growing up in His grace.

2. Indicate which of the following are works of the <u>flesh</u> rather than works of the <u>Spirit</u> by placing an **F** or **S** beside each condition. *(Refer to Galatians 5:22-23.)*

   ____ good works   ____ love   ____ intellectualism
   ____ social activism   ____ faith   ____ peace

Growing Up Together

Discuss how grace is a gift of God and cannot be purchased or earned through works. How has God's grace been exhibited in your church, and what were the results?

Growing Up to the Head!

God has extended His grace to you and expects you to do the same to others. Identify several ways you can exhibit how you are growing up to the Head by extending His grace to others.

GROWING UP TO THE HEAD

In Reconciliation

For three consecutive years it was my privilege to lead a tour group to the Holy Land. One of the highlights of the Holy Land trip was when we visited the city of Old Jerusalem.

And that he might reconcile both unto God in one body by the cross, having slain the enmity thereby. **Ephesians 2:16**

There are two Jerusalems: there is a New Jerusalem and an Old Jerusalem; and then there is the old City of David. In the city of Old Jerusalem, we got a chance to witness those of the Jewish persuasion at the Wailing Wall, as it was in Jesus' day and before. They are there right now wailing for the Ark of the Covenant that has been lost. They are wailing for the tablets, the Ten Commandments, because they don't know where they lay. They are wailing with great fervor for the coming of the Messiah, oftentimes with more fervor than do we who praise the Son of God. They are bowing down with their verbal wails as they call unto the God of their understanding. They are wailing, not believing what God has already done in Jesus.

Believers who have grown up to the Head in His reconciliation don't have to wail any more.

If we were to look at a model of Old Jerusalem, we would find that the temple there had several divisions to it. It was divided at a point where Jews could go most of the way but Gentiles could not go past a certain wall in the Temple. There was a dividing wall that Gentiles were not allowed to pass. Paul addresses this in Ephesians, as he gives us a spiritual message on the dividing wall separating Jews from Gentiles. A Gentile was anyone who was not a Jew.

Gentiles could not go beyond this wall. It was like the days of segregation in America when Blacks could not sit at the front of the bus. When I grew up in Alabama, Black people filled up the back of the bus first; White people filled up the front of the bus first. There were usually some seats in the middle in which no one sat, and that was the dividing line. And it stayed that way until the Supreme Court struck down the practice of separate but equal facilities in 1954.

> *Those who have not grown in His reconciliation are keeping themselves locked behind doors that He has already opened.*

Have you ever been kept out by a wall or a locked door? Those who have not grown in His reconciliation are keeping themselves locked behind doors that He has already opened. Think of a physical obstruction that you cannot go beyond. That's what the wall was like for Gentiles in Old Jerusalem. That's what the wall of segregation was like for Black people before public accommodation laws were passed. It was like the wall that separated God from His people before the coming of

Christ. Spiritually and theologically, Jesus tore down the wall when he died on the cross. The Romans tore down the physical wall when they destroyed the whole temple in 70 AD.

The Temple was made up of many courts. Paul focuses on the outer court, but there were really about four different courts. The outer court was where the Gentiles had to stay. Much money exchanging and selling took place in the outer court. Next, there was the court for the Jewish women. The women couldn't go any farther than this court. Even today, the men can go farther into a certain area than the women, who are still separated from the men. Christian women have been set free by the Lover of their soul who is Jesus Christ. Therefore, they are not separated from Christian men in worship. Jesus Christ was the first and great woman's Liberator. When you go still farther into the Temple, you find the Court of the Israelites. That was where the Israelite men would go and offer up sacrifices. But there was yet another inner court called the Holy of Holies. Nobody dared go into that court but the high priest, and even he could go in only once a year. Before he could enter, he had to undergo a cleansing ritual.

The Holy of Holies was separated from the rest of the Temple by a curtain. The Holy of Holies was the place where God dwelled. That is why entrance to it was restricted. The Gospels tell us that when Jesus was crucified, the curtain was torn. It's interesting to note the things Christians pay attention to with regard to the events surrounding Jesus' crucifixion, including how Mount Sinai reacted. But somehow in Christian teaching and preaching, we overlook one of the main crucifixion events. We know about the rocks splitting, we talk about how the sun darkened; but somehow we overlook the fact that when Jesus was crucified, the curtain was torn and reconciliation began. The curtain was laid apart, giving all people free access to the Father through the Great Intercessor Himself, Jesus Christ.

When famous entertainers put on a concert, they take precautions to make sure that people who don't belong backstage won't get access. Those who are an essential part of the entourage generally have a pass which reads, "all access." That lets security know that the pass holder has the right to go anywhere backstage.

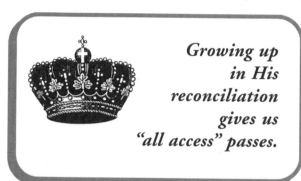

Growing up in His reconciliation gives us "all access" passes.

Growing up in His reconciliation gives us "all access" passes. We can get as close as we want to the Father, the Star of the show, because we are the priesthood of believers.

TEARING DOWN WALLS

Through His death and resurrection, Jesus broke the barrier between humanity and God. This leads me to two suppositions. First, Christ has torn down every wall that would separate humanity from God. God offers us, the world and the church, a finished and complete plan of reconciliation.

Second, we should seek to remove every obstacle, every partition, every wall that would keep a person from becoming reconciled to Christ. Sometimes churches (like the temple of Old Jerusalem) have partitions that keep worldly people, or outsiders, from coming to Jesus. Every church should grow up in His reconciliation and tear down any wall, curtain or partition that would keep a person who does not know the Lord from coming to Him. You may have seen some of those partitions in your own church, like the partition that divides people according to the kind of car they drive or how much money they make.

Before the cross (Ephesians 2:11), we were all strangers. Under the Old Covenant, we were strangers to that very covenant, strangers to the promise of God. Under the Law, we were called uncircumcised, and we had no hope for salvation or reconciliation. In the church at Ephesus, there were both Jews and Gentiles who were now bonded together by their belief that Jesus was the Messiah, the Promised One. In that one church at Ephesus, there were those who had been religious and had come up under the Jewish teaching but now confessed Christ. They were Jewish Christians (or Messianic Jews as they are known today). But the majority of the members of the church at Ephesus were Gentiles. There was quite obviously a division in thought and doctrine in the church. Those who had been circumcised under Jewish tradition teased and made mockery of those who were uncircumcised. When people join some contemporary churches, they continually are referred to as "the new members." Some of these people may have been members for many years yet they are still considered new members. They are not allowed to enter the elite circle of long-standing members.

In the church at Ephesus, the peripheral members were the uncircumcised. Circumcision was a major deal during the days of the early church. They were bickering over minutiae because they had not grown up in His reconciliation. It may be difficult for us to understand why there was such a fuss. Still, how often do we make a major deal about minor issues in the church today? The Jewish Christians made mockery of the Gentiles simply because of a little piece of skin. In verse thirteen Paul tells us, "But now in Christ Jesus you who were once far are made near by the blood of Jesus." Further, the text reads, "For he is our peace, who hath made both one, and hath broken down the middle wall of partition between us.... And that he might reconcile both unto God in one body. One body, referring to the church. One body, many members, but only one body, by the cross" (vs. 14, 16).

God not only provided a necessary channel of peace between the Jews and Gentiles, but He also broke down the wall of sin that prevents human beings from coming to Him. This really is a sin problem because whatever separates us from God is sin. Paul refers to it in the fifteenth verse as not being able to keep the law, but the problem is really about sin. Sin prevents people from coming to God. God is holy and you can't get to Him in a sinful state. You can't clean up your sins according to the law. That means without Christ, we have no hope. No one has kept the Ten Commandments all of their life. What about those commandments Jesus gave in the New Testament to fulfill the ten that God gave in the Old Testament? Who is in a position to throw the first stone? Is there one human being who is sinless? Is there any preacher or pastor anywhere who can throw the first stone? Is there a deacon in all the universe who has cause, right or righteousness to throw the first stone? None of us can do it. We can't even throw a pebble!

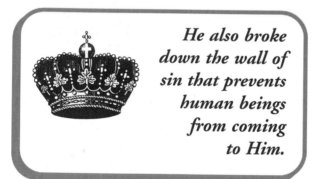

He also broke down the wall of sin that prevents human beings from coming to Him.

On our own, all by ourselves, we have no hope. We can't get to God because the wall of sin has blocked us. But Christ is our Reconciler. On the cross he dissolved the fence of sin—He tore it down. His blood bridged the gap that separated us from God. Now we have, by our faith, the grace that God has given. By grace, through faith He has allowed us to cross over. Thank God we have hope. Our hope is Jesus, who has already done what He came to do. Not only has He brought us near, but Ephesians 2:18 says He has given us access. It's one thing to get near, but it's another to get in.

Our hope is Jesus who has already done what He came to do.

Access is one of those computer terms that I have learned. I decided three or four years ago that I was not going to die illiterate in the computer realm. Anyone who plans on living for a while might as well learn about computers. Those who don't are going to be just like persons who can't read in this society. One of the first words I learned when I began operating a computer was access. I learned to turn the computer on and "boot it up," but I couldn't get in it. I have a computer in my office that can take you ever so near, but you can't access it unless you have the code. Jesus is our Access. Jesus is the Password. Jesus is the Code. The Bible says that not only is He our Access, He is the Door Opener.

Even though He is the eternal Access Code, Jesus has provided us with a companion from within Himself. We call Him the Holy Spirit. The Holy Spirit escorts us in. Jesus opens the door, and the Holy Spirit takes us by the arm and lets us come in. And when you get in, He's there to help you. He's your very present help in trouble. I thank God for what Jesus did on the cross.

Every computer needs some utilities. They help keep the computer running at its best. Utilities help keep viruses at bay. Utility software does routine maintenance checks. Utilities mend broken connections. That's what the Holy Spirit does. The Holy Spirit keeps us running at our best. He keeps us from getting spiritual viruses from other sin-sick souls. The Holy Spirit is our maintenance check. If we are worried or filled with sorrow, the Holy Spirit detects

The Holy Spirit can repair and reconcile the broken and damaged paths our lives sometimes take.

it and infuses us with God's power. The Holy Spirit mends our broken connections. Sometimes we break away from the Lord. Sometimes we break away from our family members because we have been blinded by selfishness. At times we break away from fellow Christians or church members because we've gotten our feelings hurt. The Holy Spirit can repair and reconcile the broken and damaged paths our lives sometimes take.

INVISIBLE WALLS

The curtain that was torn down at Jesus' death was a real curtain. There was a real wall in the Temple which designated the various divisions. But real walls are not the only types of barriers. Invisible walls can be even more damaging than physical walls. When there is a physical barrier, a person who wants to get on the other side begins to devise a way to get around the wall. But you can't do that with an invisible wall. An invisible wall can be dangerous because a person may not know it's there. It may be there, but you don't know how high, how wide or how thick the wall is. You may have even built walls to keep others out, not realizing that you're forcing yourself to stay in. If you can't see the wall, sometimes you don't know fully what you're up against. Growing up in reconciliation means a person is committed to picking up a sledge hammer and breaking down walls. That means personal walls, too. Some of us are afraid to take the sledge hammer to our own walls.

There are traditions made by human hands which separate people from God.

Although Jesus has given us a finished and complete plan of reconciliation, men and women continue to build walls that separate men from God, women from God, women from women, men from men, and men and women from each other. Some of the greatest battles in the church have to do with the issue of gender. There are social or class walls that separate us: the haves versus the have-nots; the upper class versus the middle class and the middle class versus the lower class. There are cultural walls that separate us. There are racial walls that separate Blacks, Whites, Asians, Hispanics, Native Americans and others. There are denominational walls that separate us—National Baptist, United Methodist, Primitive Baptist, African Methodist Episcopal, Presbyterian, Christian Methodist Episcopal, United Church of Christ, African Methodist Episcopal Zion, Southern Baptist, Lutheran, Primitive Baptist, and foot-washing Baptist, to name a few.

There are traditions made by human hands which separate people from God. God is in the business of tearing down walls, and He's going to tear them all down before it's over. It was so good for me to watch the centennial Olympic Games, which were held here in Atlanta. I was able to see some evidence of walls having been torn down in the ten or twelve years prior to the games coming to Atlanta. As I watched the opening ceremonies, it was announced that 197 nations were participating together for the first time. When I saw this I thought about the Book of Revelation. It says that He's going to gather all the nations together. It was good to see West Germany not competing against East Germany. This happened because a wall, the Berlin Wall, came tumbling down. It was good even to see the Russian team compete individually and not under the umbrella of the USSR (Union of Soviet Socialist Republics). This was possible because some walls in Russia have been torn down.

Tears came to my eyes when I saw black South Africans and white South Africans together under one flag, when just two Olympic seasons ago they were banned from coming to the Olympics because of apartheid. It was good to see our African American brothers and sisters give free expression to the joy of victory and the agony of defeat, rather than have to be bound up in the tension of a black arm band or a raised clinched fist.

Oh, what joy it gave me to watch Michael Johnson be able to cry freely as "The Star Spangled Banner" was played as he stood on the victory podium. His mentor, Jesse Owens, didn't have the freedom to cry in 1946 when Hitler refused to shake his hand. What a tremendous contrast between Johnson crying freely, as he should have, and the Olympic athletes of 1968 having to raise clinched fists. Some walls have been torn down.

LOAD-BEARING WALLS

The wall of racism still exists as a load-bearing wall, even among believers.

In the construction industry, there are "load-bearing" walls. They look the same as any other wall on the outside.

But if that wall is torn down, it can bring the whole structure down with it. Some of our greatest ills within the church and within society are resting on load-bearing walls. The wall of racism still exists as a load-bearing wall, even among believers. Just think of how many lies and fabrications would tumble down if the load-bearing wall of racism is torn down? How many myths and misconceptions would have to fall down, too? How much hatred would be dismantled if the wall of racism is no longer standing to hold up its sins?

That wall is not just one-sided either. African-Americans bash our White brothers and sisters. African-Americans don't spend nearly enough time trying to tear down our load-bearing wall of prejudice. I hear Black pastors across the country talking about White prejudice. But what about Black prejudice? Black people are as biased against Whites, Asians, Hispanics and others as Whites are against others. Let me give my African-American readers the acid test. Would you rather for your son or daughter to marry a White Christian, or would you rather they marry a Black non-Christian? Some Christians would honestly have to answer that they would prefer their child to be with a non-Christian of the same race than a Christian of a different race! God is not through with us yet. We need to open ourselves up to Him. We must avail ourselves to what He has already done. He has given us a finished plan of redemption. All we have to do is follow it.

I think we all have some responsibility for tearing down those walls. The Ephesian's Scripture is about Jews and Gentiles, but Jew and Gentile really doesn't mean anything to us. What is more pertinent to us today is Black people and White people and Brown people and Red people and Yellow people. That's the world we live in, not Jew and Gentile. As the twentieth century closes, we find ourselves living in an increasingly multicultural

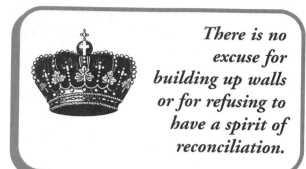

There is no excuse for building up walls or for refusing to have a spirit of reconciliation.

world, and Black people aren't adjusting to it any better than Whites or any other race, creed or color. Black people still manage to place value on insignificant matters like hair texture and skin color. We treat each other better or worse based on how much education the other has. We judge others based on the type of car or house the other person lives in.

There is some responsibility on the part of all believers in this whole matter of tearing down the walls of racism. The Supreme Court of the United States tore down some of the legal walls. Now what is left are the spiritual walls, which go much deeper than the law. The hearts of men and women will have to be changed before more walls can be torn down. The Holy Spirit will have to come in and change some folks. There is no excuse for building up walls or for refusing to have a spirit of reconciliation.

I hold to what I consider to be biblical truth—that Jesus was a Palestinian Jew. When God came in the flesh, He chose, for whatever reason, to come as a Palestinian Jew with African ancestry. God, in His awesome, divine wisdom, incarnated Himself ethnically, in sovereignly perfect fashion. According to Luke 3:23-38, God sent His Son through the lineage of Shem (v. 36). The name "Shem" means dusky or olive-colored. Interestingly, in Luke's account of the genealogy of Jesus, the male (father) gender is emphasized and not a single woman is included. This understanding is the more traditional approach. However in Matthew's account (1:1-16), four women are mentioned who are of Hamitic (African) descent—namely, Tamar,

Rahab, Ruth and Bathsheba. Therefore, based on Scripture, ethnically speaking, Jesus was a *mestizo*—a person with mixed ancestry.

... God is too smart to exclude Himself ethnically or in any other way from any people or person.

Again, the historical Jesus was not what we currently classify as European. He was primarily Semitic with African ancestry. Today, however, Semitic people are usually classified as Caucasian (White). So in the divine genealogy of the eternal God—the historical, incarnate God—Jesus can be claimed by all as Savior, Friend and elder Brother. Jesus can be claimed ethnically by people of Semitic, Hamitic and Caucasian descent. When we have grown up to the Head in reconciliation, we will realize that God is too smart to exclude Himself ethnically or in any other way from any people or person. While I believe that, I'm almost scared to preach on its sometimes because some of us are so biased in our thinking that it fuels fires of racism. Discussing issues of race seem to give some people permission to see the world totally from a racial perspective.

African-Americans must take ownership in the need for growing up in His reconciliation where racial issues are concerned. We need to be careful with the word Afrocentric. We need to be careful with the word Eurocentric. The word centric means "center of." The Bible says that Christ is the Chief Cornerstone. Africa cannot be the chief cornerstone. Europe cannot be the chief cornerstone. The United States of America cannot be the chief cornerstone. Christocentric, or Christ-centered, is the only way we can be.

When Jesus created a new personhood, He made a new being, one body, the Church. He did not raise Gentiles up to be even with Jews. He did not raise Black people up to be equal with White, or White to be equal with Black. What He did was melt them all down and raise up a new being. One person, one body, one baptism, one Spirit.

There are even walls of denominationalism. I once was privileged to preach at an African Methodist Episcopal Church (AME) district conference. The bishop who invited me had heard my presentation at the Hampton Ministers' Conference, which is held every year at Hampton University in Hampton, Virginia. I made history, and he made history. I was the first non-AME to ever lecture and preach at one of their conferences in Georgia. The bishop was applauded for stepping beyond the line to invite a non-AME.

A good friend of mine preached beautifully at Greenforest, but he cannot invite me to preach at his church because I'm not Unitarian (Oneness) Assembly Pentecostal. Yet we both are supposed to be members of Christian churches. Walls of denominationalism divide good Christians and prevent fellowship and praise to the one true God. Many of us argue about beliefs and doctrines over which we have no control anyway. We are divided over premillenialism versus postmillenialism versus amillenialism. Others of us think we have got the inside secret to the kingdom—that other believers won't go to heaven because everybody else outside of themselves is wrong. So many of the things which divide Christians are based on human belief and preference, not divine revelation. How much Christian fellowship has been lost? How much has the kingdom of God suffered? How much evil has run amuck, all because Christians are somewhere arguing over denominational issues? That division can cross over denominations, or it can be intradenominational.

Baptists seem to be particularly susceptible to this—perhaps this is due to the Baptist belief in local autonomy. Each church may have the right to govern itself, but that creates a

Walls of tradition separate us and keep people from coming to God.

fertile ground for dissension on a denominational level. We need to distinguish when we are taking a true stand concerning doctrinal issues and when we are simply arguing over denominational preferences.

Walls of tradition separate us and keep people from coming to God. How many of you have ever frowned at someone in your church because of the way that person was dressed? How many older Christians have turned up their noses to Christian rap music? How many are fighting to hold on to meaningless church traditions simply because "it's always been that way"? Some people are even fighting to hold on to traditions that are oppressive or counterproductive. Yet we hold on to those traditions—we fight for them. We are even willing to leave a church for them! How many of us would fight so strongly or would hold so dearly to Christ Himself?

But here is the acid test for our hearts and our minds—What is our understanding of the word sacred? There is nothing sacred in God's eyesight except the Gospel of Jesus Christ. The pulpit itself is not sacred. There is nothing sacred about a Baldwin organ, a pipe organ or a Hammond organ. While some people really get upset when the communion table is used for any other purpose, the table itself is not sacred. There is nothing sacred about an altar itself; it's just wood. There is

God is calling the church of today to break down the walls of racism, tradition, denominationalism, or any obstacle that would prevent a person from coming to God.

no such thing as a sacred music tempo either. Is there something in the tempo of "religious" music that is more sacred than any other tempo? That is nowhere in the Bible, nor is it even inferred. We put up a wall and say that certain music should not be in church because it has an "unsacred tempo." A younger, newer generation is going to hell, in part, because we have put a sacred tradition on tempo.

God is calling the church of today to break down the walls of racism, tradition, denominationalism, or any obstacle that would prevent a person from coming to God. God has given us a complete plan, a finished plan of salvation. Many of us came to Christ through the tempo of the music in our world today. Some of our most beloved church songs are melodies taken from the secular world. Is an unsaved, or lost, person going to listen to a radio station that has organ music on it? Turn your radio to whatever secular station you listen to and see if you find any organ music. As Christians we have to ask ourselves if our actions indicate that we want people to get saved? That's our purpose.

The only thing that is sacred is the old rugged cross. The dangerous, awesome message of the rugged cross of Jesus who died and suffered in our stead is sacred. The cross is sacred because it was there that He suffered, died and bled so that humanity would be reconciled unto Him. God so loved an unsaved generation, an unsaved world—not the church—that He tore down the wall and bridged the gap, giving free accessibility to everybody in and through the great Intercessor and Advocate, our Lord and Savior, Jesus Christ. God tore down the wall to build up the church, not to divide it.

> *A church that is not growing is out of obedience with the teaching of the Bible and the desire of God.*

RECONCILING AND GROWING

How can we possibly reap the harvest unless we are willing to gather all the crop? If we are workers in the field, we cannot choose to pick only tomatoes and step over the cabbage and okra. We must pick all the harvest that is ripe to be gathered. That is how the kingdom grows. God wants and expects the Church to grow in number as well as in spirit. A church that is not growing is out of obedience with the teaching of the Bible and the desire of God. You cannot have a little tea party and continue to edify yourself just because a certain number of people arrived.

God expects the church to grow. In Ephesians 2:21-22 we find, "In whom all the building fitly framed together groweth unto an holy temple in the Lord: In whom ye also are builded together for an habitation of God through the Spirit." Two major dynamics are right within those verses. The first is that the church must bring new stones to be fit into the building. The stones will be all types, shapes and sizes. Some will be so dirty you may not want to touch them. Our job as workers is not to judge the fitness of the stones. We can't look at a particular stone and declare, "That stone can't possibly be cleaned up." We've got to simply bring them first; that's part of the purpose of the church, to gather new stones. When was the last time you brought a stone to the church? When was the last time you brought an irreligious person to church? When was the last time you brought a believer or unbeliever into the

When is the last time you brought an irreligious person to church?

building? When have you added to or reinforced the building by gathering stones? Are you simply coming yourself saying, "I want to be edified, and if I'm not edified it's the choir's fault or the preacher's fault because they didn't get me filled up."

After you bring them in you've got to shape them to fit in, that's the second purpose. Every believer is a laborer, not just the preacher, the deacons and the ministerial staff; every believer is a laborer who is expected to be adding to the building. Every believer has to help polish stones. That takes work. Some stones need a little more work than others. Some stones will take up your time so much until you wonder if it's worth the effort.

Peter tells us we are living stones. Our Savior, Jesus Christ, is the Chief Cornerstone, and we are living stones. We are supposed to bring, shape and add because we're building a habitation. If you were building your own house, would you want dirty, misshapen, unpolished stones to be used? Would you want stones that had been carelessly polished, used to hold up the exterior of your home? Why, then, would we do any less for God's edifice—the Church?

He has torn down the walls and formed us to be a Church, and that Church is one body. At the cross Christ dissolved the wall and built the bridge. He didn't build one church for Blacks and another for Whites and still another for Asians, Hispanics or Native Americans. He didn't create one church for poor folks and another for the middle class. There is not one church for sacred organ music and one for more rhythmic sounds. The church is not just for those who fall out in the aisles nor simply for those who maintain their composure in worship.

Those are all human preferences. God has no preferences except that we give Him our highest. God has no walls. Walls make us comfortable because our minds and our spirits are small. God is too big for walls. We want to build walls to contain God so that we can understand Him, but God doesn't work like that. We have to tear down our internal walls so that we may know Him and experience Him in His fullness.

> *God has no walls. Walls make us comfortable because our minds and our spirits are small. God is too big for walls.*

APPLICATION

What does reconciliation have to do with spiritual and numerical growth? First, take a personal inventory. Look in the mirror and evaluate yourself. Think of prejudices and biases as walls. Be honest with yourself ... think of a bias that you have against a particular group of people. Imagine that bias as a wall. It blocks you from loving God's other children. It stops you from knowing them as fellow Christians. Maybe your bias even stops you from wanting some person or group to be saved, especially if you're going to have to be the one to present the Gospel to them.

Think very hard about yourself. Have you built up a wall against ministering to homosexuals, for example? Would you let a person die and go to hell simply because you refuse to present God's plan of salvation to that one person? Would you refuse to give help to a man dying of AIDS because he is a homosexual or a drug

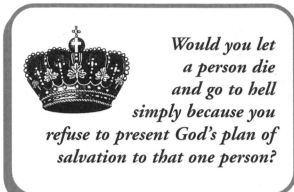

Would you let a person die and go to hell simply because you refuse to present God's plan of salvation to that one person?

addict? If so, ask yourself if God is going to ask you about that come Judgement Day.

A prominent African-American preacher once told a story about the night he and his wife got all dressed up to attend a theatrical production. As they waited for a traffic light to change so they could cross the street, he noticed a shabbily dressed, perhaps intoxicated Black man on the other side. Standing there in his tuxedo, the preacher thought to himself, "Please don't let this man say anything to me. Not in the midst of all these theatre-going White people." As circumstance would have it, the man did address the preacher as they were crossing the street. The preacher pretended to ignore his comments. As the well-dressed preacher and his wife walked past, the hobo shouted back, "I love you, man." Humbled, the preacher said after all these years he still believes he will meet that man in heaven. For, in his classism and superficiality, he— a man of God—missed an opportunity to show love toward "the least of these." Yet, the "least of these" knew how to show love for him.

Jonah had a wall built up, blocking him from caring about the people of Nineveh. He didn't want to go over there to save those people, even though God had told him to! He had to spend three days in a fish's belly before his stubbornness could be turned around. Some people are in a spiritual fish's belly right now because they have built up a wall which blocks them from

> *What will it take for your wall to be torn down so that you can grow up to the Head in reconciliation?*

doing God's work and are unwilling to tear it down. What will it take for your wall to be torn down so that you can grow up to the Head in reconciliation?

Some of us have walls, and some of those walls are "load-bearing." You know you have a load-bearing wall if your life is structured on the sin that made up that wall. For example, in years gone by, many White Christians held load-bearing walls of racism. Their entire understanding of God and the order of the universe rested on the belief that they were superior and that Blacks were inferior. By the grace of God many of them allowed their load-bearing walls to be torn down.

Many in the Nation of Islam, especially those in the original Nation, lived with load-bearing walls. They believed that Whites were devils and that salvation did not lie within Christ. Their frustration with a racist society caused them to construct load-bearing walls of hatred and prejudice against Whites. After a time, many Blacks came to or returned to Christianity, allowing Christ to demolish the load-bearing wall. Growing up in His reconciliation means giving our load-bearing wall to Him.

Christ has to tear down our load-bearing walls if He is to have us completely. We have to deny our old self, our old structure so the Master Builder can build us anew. Sometimes it takes time to tear down our own walls which we have fortified over the years. If you

Growing up in His reconciliation forces us to tear down all walls.

have a wall, take it to Jesus. He specializes in breaking them down. With His holy "wrecking ball," He will crumble our barriers to wholeness. But He will only do it if we ask Him.

Some walls, while not load-bearing, are walls nevertheless. Growing up in His reconciliation forces us to tear down all walls. They block God's love and our own spiritual growth. For example, many "righteous" Christians have had walls built up against divorced people until their own child became a victim of divorce. Others turned their back on the AIDS community until someone they loved deeply was stricken with the disease. Some fine, devout White Christians were quite comfortable in their prejudices against Blacks until their son or daughter married a Black person and gave them half-Black grandchildren. For most of these people, their love for what is part of their own blood helped them to rise above their wall of bias.

Every wall has a weak spot. Sometimes God has to pick away at the weak spot in our walls in order to break them down. In a short story by Stephen King entitled "Rita Hayworth and the Shawshank Redemption," a man is falsely convicted of murdering his wife. One day as he chiseled his name on the wall of his prison cell, he discovered a weak spot. Over the next twenty years, the man bored through that wall until he broke free.

It is quite possible for us to go through this Christian walk with our walls fully intact. Then why bother to tear them down? When we live with walls, we can never become what Jesus fully intended for us to be. When we live with walls, we block the fullness of who God is.

Having accepted that walls hinder your spiritual growth, ask yourself how your spiritual walls are affecting the life of your church? Are your

The church is only as healthy and open as its members.

walls, combined with the various walls of others in your church, blocking kingdom growth as well? Is it not possible for a poor person to join your church? A person of another race or culture? A person who has led, or is leading, a particular lifestyle? If you think your walls are only affecting you, think again.

The church is only as healthy and open as its members. Think about your church's level of openness. Is your church one which freely and openly accepts anyone who wants to enter its doors. Does your church freely and joyfully accept anyone who genuinely wants to be a part of the body? Have you contributed to blocking the growth of your church and of God's kingdom because of your walls?

FOR STUDY AND REVIEW

Chapter Three
Growing Up to the Head in His Reconciliation

1. What is the definition of reconciliation?

2. The most inner court was known as the _____ of _____. It was separated from the rest of the temple by a _____.

3. During the crucifixion of Christ, the curtain separating sinful humanity from a Holy God was torn from _____ to _____.

4. Growing up in His reconciliation give us "all access" passes. This is called the _____ of the _____.

5. By referring to people who join the church as "new members" for at least one year, this gives them the feeling of being "distinguished," full members. True _____ or False _____.

6. Consider whether you have allowed racism to build a "load-bearing" wall around you. What is the first step that you need to take in allowing the Lord to tear down that wall?

Growing Up in His Word

1. Re-read the entire Book of Ephesians, focusing on 2:11-22. Who are the Gentiles Paul was speaking about? Why were they considered Gentiles? What separated them from God? What action reconciled them back to God?

2. What is the spiritual temple referred to in Ephesians 2:19-22? Explain your answer.

Growing Up Together

1. List several "isms" evident within churches which build walls that cause division.

2. What are some things a church can do to ensure it is identified as being a church "without walls"?

Growing Up to the Head!

Since Christ has reconciled us back to God through the tearing down of walls that separate, any walls in our lives that keep us from growing up to the Head are human-made.

(a) Identify any human-made walls in your life that are stifling your growth.

(b) What are your plans for having these walls demolished?

GROWING UP TO THE HEAD

In His Purpose

God's history with Israel is an example of obstacles to His purpose. It was after thousands of years and many broken covenants that God's plan was re-

According to the eternal purpose which he purposed in Christ Jesus our Lord.

Ephesians 3:11

vealed. Ephesians 3:7-11 explains that God had His plan and purpose all along, even though He did not reveal it beforehand. One may ask why God did not reveal His plan to Adam and Eve or to Israel or the Prophets. Even though the prophets of the Old Testament were given revelations, no one knew exactly what God had in mind.

When the stakes are high, it is generally better to keep the plans secret. During the years of the Cold War with the Soviet Union, our government determined that it was essential to keep certain information secret. Now that the threat of Communism has all but expired, much of that information has been released. After the Freedom of Information Act was passed, many documents which were once top secret were released for public review. But only documents which are determined to have no effect on national security can be released. God needed to keep His perfect plan hidden until the proper time for release. In the 3rd Chapter of Ephesians, the writer also marvels over God's purpose for the Church.

GOD'S PURPOSE FOR THE CHURCH

Contrary to how some churches may operate, God has a purpose for the Church. God has gifted His Church for His purpose. Yet, many local churches may not be operating in accordance with that purpose. In fact, they may not have a biblical clue as to what they are supposed to be doing.

A survey was done to determine the number of Christians who knew the biblical purpose of the church. The sad commentary was that only three out of ten pastors of mainline churches today knew the biblical purpose of the Church. If the number of clergy was that low, imagine where the laypersons fell in the survey. Actually, they weren't that far behind. Only one out of ten church members knew the purpose of the church as God has given it in the Bible.

> *God has charged us with a five-fold purpose: worship, fellowship, discipleship, evangelism and ministry/service.*

God has charged us with a five-fold purpose: worship, fellowship, discipleship, evangelism and ministry/service. We have been gifted for the task of fulfilling His purpose. Given that so few people, both clergy and laity alike, know the purpose of the Church as outlined in the Bible, it is little wonder there is so much discontent in our churches.

The reason we Christians individually and collectively have no joy and no peace is because we have no purpose. When unfulfilled people come together, they form unfulfilled groups. A church filled with discontent people will be a discontent church. We Christians ought to be as content as the Carnation milk cow that was once on television. That Carnation cow was very content. The reason we have no contentment and are filled with anxiety is that we have not grown up to His purpose. Living to fulfill God's purpose is the key to being fruitful and fulfilled.

God has called us to be fruitful, and He's called us to be fulfilled. When we have a purpose, we have joy and peace, and our life has meaning. Many people spend their entire lifetime trying to discover their purpose. Some people never find it. But the search for purpose is simple. In order to find our purpose, we have to find out what Jesus' purpose was. When we find Jesus' agenda and we join His agenda, we have real purpose. The Bible says Jesus came to seek and to save. Somehow, we the church, have to find our purpose in that purpose. In other words, everything we do as a church should lead to seeking and to challenging others to get saved. Growing up in His purpose means directing our lives in order to seek and share the saving knowledge of Jesus Christ.

> *Growing up in His purpose means directing our lives in order to seek and share the saving knowledge of Jesus Christ.*

A PICTURE OF THE CHURCH

I want to share with you three pictures which will lend further insight into the purpose of the church. What is God saying to us about the purpose of the Church? The first picture is found in the first two verses of the 15th Chapter of the Gospel of Luke: "Then drew nigh unto Him the publicans and the sinners to hear Him. And the Pharisees and the scribes murmured saying, this man receiveth sinners and eateth with them." I'm not an artist, so I can't draw a physical picture of what I'm trying to convey. But if I were to draw a picture, based on this text, it would be called, "The Church in Her Ignorance." Maybe if an actual picture were drawn, it would be a church with its steeple made to look like a dunce cap. Here you have Jesus in a major confrontation with the religious people of His day. They were ignorant to the purpose of Jesus and what he was all about. In their ignorance they complained to Jesus, mocked and criticized Him because He associated with sinners ... publicans. He went to dinner at a sinner's house. He sat and talked at length with an adulteress. He let a woman with a bad reputation touch him and put expensive perfume on His feet. The religious "church" people wondered, "What's wrong with this man?" The reactions of these people emphasizes the fact that it is possible to be religious yet not a Christian.

Often, I hear people talk about their family and their spouses. They say, "You know, he's a very religious man." But I have to ask, "Is he a Christian?" There's a lot of difference between being religious and being a Christian. Here in this picture is the religious world in its ignorance. The Bible does not say that God so loved the *church*, but that's the way church people

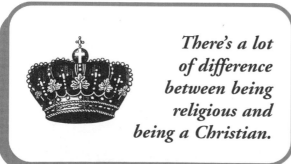

There's a lot of difference between being religious and being a Christian.

want to act. John 3:16 says God loved the *world* so much He gave His only Son. Christians need to start loving the world enough to get the world saved. That doesn't mean we need to love worldly

The Bible does not say that God so loved the church, but that's the way church folk want to act.

ways. We don't need to love sinful ways. We need to reach out to non-Christians, the unchurched, the non-religious. We need to reach out to them because we, like the Father, love them enough to want them to go to heaven, too.

Too often church people try to contain God under lock and key within the walls of the church. Sometimes clergy and other religious leaders want to believe that God only speaks to them. In the movie, "Oh, God," John Denver plays a grocery store manager who, at best, is agnostic. God reveals Himself to Denver's character in physical form. God, portrayed by George Burns, tells Denver to call together some of the religious leaders of the day. All these religious men scoffed at the possibility of God speaking to a mere grocery store employee. One southern televangelist was particularly indignant, thinking God surely would have chosen him to reveal His divine message. Likewise, the religious leaders of Jesus' day were upset, thinking surely God would not reveal Himself through a mere carpenter.

The second picture is really a combination of the parables of the lost sheep and of the lost coin (Luke 15:4-10). In both of these pictures, one of many is lost: one sheep out of 100; one coin out of ten. In both parables, what was lost or missing was considered important enough to stop everything and go look for it. The one missing possession, in each case, was not dismissed and forgotten because it was gone. The one lost sheep was important enough for the shepherd to leave the ninety-nine and go look for it. The one lost coin was important enough for the woman to light a candle and sweep or canvass the floor to find it. Has the church done this? Have we engaged in an unending search for those who are lost? Perhaps if this were an actual drawing, it would be a picture of a church with hands covering its eyes, playing a game of hide and seek. Except in this case, the count has gone to ten, and the church has not un-

> *In some churches, members act like they are doing the lost a personal favor by allowing them to enter.*

covered her eyes. In the parable, once the owner has found the lost possession, there is rejoicing and celebration. The man put the sheep on his shoulder and just started rejoicing. He couldn't even wait until he got back to tell someone. Now that's real joy. Has your rejoicing ever been so great that you didn't know and didn't care who saw you? When the woman found her coin, she was so excited she had to go tell somebody. How often does the church rejoice over lost coins and lost sheep?

In some churches, members act like they are doing the lost a personal favor by allowing them to enter. An interracial couple began visiting a White church in a mid-sized southern city. After a few weeks the pastor suggested that perhaps they would feel more comfortable worshiping at the evening service. The wife, an African-American, was devastated. When she mentioned the incident to some of her Sunday School class members, they reminded her that in some parts of the city, churches would not have welcomed them at all. That young couple was looking for a place to worship, and the church thought it was doing the couple a favor. The church people thought the couple should have been rejoicing when it was really the other way around. The church should have been rejoicing over a lost interracial couple looking for a church home.

But churches are confused, and not just on the issue of interracial marriage. More often than not, churches are not seeking the lost. They are closing their eyes and turning their backs. Occasionally, if someone stumbles upon them, they will allow that one in if he or she fits the church's standards. When I look at those two parables, they both conclude the same way, "likewise," as in likewise is the kingdom of heaven...likewise is the kingdom of God ... likewise is the family of God ... likewise is the church.

In Ephesians, the third picture may not easily be seen. But a great artist can see things on a blank canvas that no one else can. I am not claiming to be a great artist, but I want to show you what I see. Ephesians 8:4 reads, "Wherefore he saith, When he ascended up on high, he led captivity captive, and gave gifts unto men." I see a picture when I continue reading the fourth chapter, "(Now that he ascended, what is it but that he also descended first into the lower parts of the earth? He that descended is the same also that ascended up far above all heavens, that he might fill all things.)"

Now let me share my picture of a king who's been to war. He's been in a bloody battle. He's been in a hard war. But the king comes riding on his victory stallion ... riding into victory ... riding his black beauty. Behind him is his army, and they are rejoicing. Bringing up the rear are the captives, those over whom the king has won the battle. They are now in bondage with handcuffs and chains. The captives have come out of battle

Growing up in His purpose means growing up in His gifts.

whipped. They look beaten. They are bloodied, worn down and defeated. They come staggering into the camp. Then the king turns around and gives the victory to the people in the form of a gift. The king is the victor. God almighty is the One who rode into battle.

If this were a religious picture, it would be the king riding in on his stallion. Behind him are his people, his loyal subjects and soldiers, carrying the church on their shoulders. The king does not have to look back because he knows his subjects are carrying on with the church, that which has been entrusted to them.

If you understand who the enemy is, you will get a clearer image of the picture. Who are those who have come into bondage? Let me tell you who the enemy is. Separation is the enemy ... sin is the enemy ... death is the enemy ... alienation is the enemy. The point is that God has gone to war on our behalf, and He has conquered all the enemies that would make life useless and meaningless.

GIFTED FOR THE TASK

Growing up in His purpose means growing up in His gifts. Not only does He save us but He gifts us. He saves us, not just *from* something, but also *for* something. Too many Christians think it all stops at salvation. Some of us think, "I'm saved, it's all done now. I'll come to church pretty regularly and sooner or later I'm going to heaven." We want to stop the process at the point of receiving salvation. Salvation (accepting Christ), however, is just the beginning of our Christian walk. The scriptural mandate is that He has gifted every Christian for a task. Why, then, is the church sometimes so purposeless? Why, then, do we lack joy? Why do we have no peace? Why have we no contentment? Why are we filled with so much anxiety? Why does conflict abound in the church? It's all because we have not grown up to His purpose.

Why does conflict abound in the church? It's all because we have not grown up to His purpose.

If we who claim to be His disciples would join Christ in His agenda and not our own, we wouldn't have conflict in the church. If we would all yield ourselves to His purpose and not our own, miracles would occur in our ministries. Imagine what would happen if we would drive to the church's business meetings praying all the way, "Thy will be done, not mine...." It's hard to have conflict on the deacon board if every deacon is joined into Christ's purpose for the church. It's hard to have conflict in the choir if everybody who joined sang with God's purpose in mind. If we fully commit ourselves—I mean totally commit—to this task, we will overcome. Many of us are Christians but we are not totally committed. We're not totally committed to the purpose of the church. Pastors can make an appeal for members to come to Sunday School, but the members aren't going to come because they're not committed enough to get up! In fact, many church people think Sunday School is for children. Many adults think they have graduated with a Ph.D. in Bible learning; they've gotten a culminating degree from the Word of God, and they don't need to go to Bible study. When we have this type of attitude, we've missed the whole point. When we think like that, we will not be able to minister to other persons. God has gifted us to minister to each other. God's got plenty of people for us to minister to. But most of us are not totally committed. We're not committed to sacrificial service.

Growing up in His purpose means growing up in sacrificial service. Sacrifice always means you've got to give up something. We've got to give up something to come to Wednesday night Bible study. Instead, some of us use that time to cut the grass,

Growing up in His purpose means growing up in sacrificial service.

watch HBO or go to a party. What about on Sunday morning? Most of us don't go to church at 9:30 a.m. or 9:45 a.m. for Sunday School. We'll get to church about 11:30 a.m. or

11:45 a.m. because that's when the preacher's about ready to get up. A good many church members do just enough to ease their conscience and say they've been to church.

In the survey I referenced earlier, what most church members actually said was that they perceive the purpose of the church to be that of "taking care of *my* needs." We want to come to church to get *our* needs met. Every church should be about meeting the needs of its members. But if everyone comes to get his or her needs met, who's going to do the needs-meeting? If everyone only comes to get his or her needs met, then everybody in the church is going to be standing around saying, "What about me?" Growing up in His purpose means allowing His love to shine through you so that you can be a "needs-meeter." As God is a "Way-Maker," we will be His "needs-meeters." The Way-Maker does not leave His people poorly staffed or equipped for His purpose. We do not serve a welfare God. We

> *Growing up in His purpose means knowing that He will give us everything we need as we need it in order to do His will.*

do not serve a stingy God. We serve an able God. Growing up in His purpose means knowing that He will give us everything we need as we need it in order to do His will.

I want to share with you a few things about the gifts He has given you so that you can accomplish His purpose. Verse seven in the fourth Chapter of Ephesians states that every believer is gifted: "But unto every one of us is given grace according to the measure of the gift of Christ." There are no Christians or believers who are not gifted. Every believer has been given a gift! The question is, What is your gift? If you know what your gift is, are you using it (or them)? If you aren't, why not?

Verses eight and ten remind us that every believer's gift has been paid for with a price: Christ's experiencing hell on the cross. He paid for this gift. I don't just mean He died on the cross for our salvation, though He did. The Scripture says that He who ascended is the same one who descended. Somewhere between Friday night and early Sunday morning He had some work to do. On Friday night He went down to Sheol, Hades, to set the captives free. He went down there to give us our gift.

In every believer's gift is a three-fold purpose. It is explained in Ephesians 4:15: first, perfecting the saints; second, the work of ministry; and third, edifying the body of Christ. Sometimes in the church we say it differently: evangelize the sinner, equip the saints and exalt the Savior. It's the same as, "Find them, bring them in, grow them up." No matter how we say it, we have been gifted for the task.

FIND, BRING, GROW, SEND

The purpose statement of the church where I serve as pastor, Greenforest Community Baptist Church, can be summarized thusly: "The purpose of the church is to find them, bring them in, grow them up and send them out." God tells us to "find them, bring them in, and grow them up." We learned about sentences like this in school—sentences where the subject is not given but implied. A sentence like this is considered a command. In the English language, the subject is always understood to be "you." So, God is really saying, "(You) Find them, (you) bring them in, and (you) grow them up." But churches act like the subject is "I." They think either God is supposed to do it or the preacher is. The implied "you" means every one who claims to follow Him. If we do that, it will keep us busy. We won't have time for gossip because we're too busy looking for lost souls. We won't have time for judging because time is precious and there are too many lost souls to find. We won't have time to stir up mess and conflict in the church because we've got souls to look for.

God has greater things in mind for His people. He did not create us to stir up conflict and confusion. That is for the lost. The redeemed are supposed to be removed from that. This is what it means to be sanctified—"separated or set apart." When He has set you apart, you

Growing up in His purpose means putting personal agendas aside to make room for His divine plans.

should not go back dipping into the pettiness He brought you out of. Growing up in His purpose means putting personal agendas aside to make room for His divine plans.

FIND THEM

First, we've got to find them, seek them out like the golden egg at an egg hunt. In many egg hunts, there is one egg hidden that is really special. Sometimes it's painted gold or some other unusual color. That's the egg you really want. That's the egg that wins the money or the prize. Every lost soul should be treated like a prize waiting to be found. Every lost soul is a golden egg.

For ages children have played hide-and-seek. Well, the lost souls are hiding and many church folk haven't uncovered their eyes so they can go look for them. We ought to be saying, "Ready or not, world, here we come looking for you." Every believer ought to be able to switch his or her name with my name in that sentence. Every church ought to be saying, "Look out lost souls, Greenforest Baptist Church (or your church) is coming to get you. You can hide if you want to, but we're not going to stop looking until we find you!"

His giftedness to us should enable us to keep looking, always seeking new and different places to find lost souls. We're on God's winning team. We're on the championship team and we should not forget it.

> *His giftedness to us should enable us to keep looking, always seeking new and different places to find lost souls.*

BRING THEM IN

After we find them, we've got to bring them in. When we bring them in, the only proper response is to rejoice. Every found soul is cause for celebration. Just like the father celebrated when the prodigal son returned home, we should be partying in the church house every time somebody walks down the aisle! The windows should be rattling, and the doors should be shaking because we

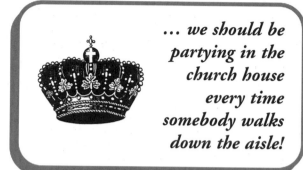

... we should be partying in the church house every time somebody walks down the aisle!

are rocking the church house with praise.

Whoever comes down the aisle for whatever reason—whether it's the first time or the fifth time; whether they're coming to get salvation or a booster shot from backsliding; whether they're coming from another church or even from Bedside Baptist Church—no matter the reason, we ought to be rejoicing because a decision has been made to live out a life for Christ. When someone comes down the aisle, some of us are more interested in the ham and sweet potatoes waiting for us at home than the wandering soul who just came down the aisle.

GROW THEM UP

Once we bring them in, we have to help them grow up. It is every Christian's duty to grow up. Salvation is not a line you cross over, it is a process. Ephesians 4:15 reads, "But speaking the truth in love, may (we) grow up into him in all things, which is the head, even Christ." Let me paint a picture of this. The picture is of the church. Christ is the Head and His believers are the body.

As I stated in the Introduction, my head, once a source of ridicule, is now a source of glory. People in Atlanta now know me by my distinctive head of white hair. If I put a cap on in winter, people hardly know me. What I used to want to hide, I now want to show off. God is in the business of transformation. He's in the metamorphosis business. His giftedness to us should enable us to keep looking, always seeking new and different places to find lost souls. He's in the business of taking something ugly and making it beautiful. He's in the business of making you and me all over again. That's what salvation does. When we are saved, we are His diamonds-in-the-rough. If we let Him, He will work with us, shape us and polish us until we become beautiful and brilliant. There is not a more beautiful sight than seeing someone who used to be doing everything in the world but who is now a dedicated soldier in the Army of the Lord.

Have you ever heard someone testify about how they were delivered? If we've been delivered, a testimony like that gives Christians goose bumps because it makes us remember how we used to be. If we let Him, God takes us and makes us into someone we don't even recognize. Christians are called to grow up. Christ is calling for His Church to grow up. Growing up to His purpose is just part of the growth process. Growing up to His purpose means having the willingness

Christ is calling for His Church to grow up.

to be molded and shaped so that we can do His will. Isaiah 64:8 says, "But now, O LORD, thou art our father; we are the clay, and thou our potter; and we all are the work of thy hand."

In Jeremiah 18:6, the Lord is asking, "Why can't I even do with you what a potter does with a piece of clay?" He asked Jeremiah,

People have to grow into knowing what God has purposed for them.

"O house of Israel, cannot I do with you as this potter? saith the LORD. Behold, as the clay is in the potter's hand, so are ye in mine hand, O house of Israel." Growing up to His purpose means knowing we belong to Him and not ourselves. Growing up to His purpose means being as clay in the Potter's hands.

DISCIPLING BELIEVERS

No church can think its job is done if it just finds people and brings them in, though many churches do just that. One young pastor had a church that would boast his accomplishments each year during the pastor's anniversary. Every year they would tell how, under his leadership, at least 300 people had come to Christ. After five years, that church should have had at least 1500 more members. But the church wasn't really growing. They were finding folks and bringing them in, but they fell short in the mandate to grow them so they could be sent out to bring in others. Consequently, many new converts in that church "fell by the wayside."

For true church growth to occur, there must be a growth mechanism in place. Would you hire someone for a new job and just sit them at a desk and tell them to get to work? What would that new worker do? After a while, he or she would probably quit and find a new job where someone provided some on-the-job training. We have to help grow people up so that they grow up to His purpose. People have to grow into knowing what God has purposed for them. If we don't help, we haven't done our job. It is one of the responsibilities of the church, to implement a discipleship training ministry to help believers discern their spiritual gifts and how God wants them to be used. Once a believer dis-

> *If believers are not properly trained ... they may wander through the church, actually doing more harm than good.*

covers his or her gifts, the church has a responsibility to train him or her in using those gifts properly. People need to be trained to understand that their spiritual gifts come from God, not from themselves. People need to be trained to understand that they are accountable to God for the appropriate use of those gifts. People need to be trained so they do not develop a "prima dona" mentality, thinking that the church will not survive without them or their gifts.

If believers are not properly trained concerning spiritual gifts, they may wander through the church, actually doing more harm than good. Our churches are often remiss in helping people discern their gifts. More often, we are simply looking for warm bodies to fill empty slots. To allow people to work anywhere in the church, without regard, is contradictory to spiritual gifts. In 1 Corinthians 12, Paul tells us that the same Spirit gives us different gifts. That means everybody is not meant to be an usher, a preacher, a youth minister, a refreshments committee member or a preschool Sunday School teacher. Often, a good indicator of a spiritual gift is when the person has an inordinate, or higher than average, interest in that ministry. In other words, the person is usually called to the ministry they have a passion for. People who dis-

The church must take the initiative to direct this process in the lives of the membership.

play strong feelings of concern for the plight of youth generally have a calling to youth ministry. People who feel strongly about how people, especially visitors, are greeted at the church doors usually have a calling to usher. The church must take the initiative to direct this process in the lives of the membership.

The church has to grow members up to become deacons, Sunday School teachers, ushers, choir members, and youth ministers. We have to grow them up because they don't come in knowing that they are babes in Christ. The average person will not volunteer to look stupid. Does your church have trouble finding Sunday School teachers? Youth workers? What about choir members? Musicians? Keep seeking them and bringing them, but start growing them, too. God may have what you need already sitting in your church yet nobody, including that person, knows it. Have you ever found out someone in your church could sing, lead others, play an instrument, organize an event, or motivate others but nobody was aware of it? If we don't grow them up, nobody will ever know. Think of the potential gone to waste! We are charged. Grow them up to His purpose.

SEND THEM OUT

When a potter finishes his work, he wants to put it out to be displayed or sold. In other words, the potter does his work for a reason. The Master Potter has a reason for His work with us. God saves us, molds us, cleans us up and shapes us for His purpose. God works in each of us a masterpiece so that we can go out and bring in other lumps of clay which need to be shaped and molded. In Job 23:10, God's servant says, "But he knoweth the way that I take: when he hath tried me, I shall come forth as gold." When God does His divine alchemy and turns us from something worthless to something precious, we need to go out and tell it. When we have been through the fire and come out, we shouldn't have to be sent. We really should be glad to go because like the old song says, "I couldn't keep it to myself, what the Lord has done for me..."

When God does His divine alchemy and turns us from something worthless to something precious, we need to go out and tell it.

How many churches in your city actually send their folk out to do witnessing? How many churches actually have a program in place to reach the unsaved and the unchurched? Has your church even sent out a letter inviting someone to visit your church? Has your church ever tried to find out about the new people who have moved into your town or your neighborhood? How many churches can you name that actually train their people and send them out? Most churches, even evangelical churches, talk a lot about those who need to be saved but don't really do much about it. They don't bring people in with the idea of sending them out. Some folks are occupying space on a church pew right now, just waiting to be sent. They are waiting for the charge. They are waiting for their church to fire the starter pistol so they can go. Sound the charge! It's time to send them out!

God saves us for a reason. In Matthew 5:14-16, Jesus tells us, "Ye are the light of the world. A city that is set on an hill cannot be hid. Neither do men light a candle, and put it under a bushel, but on a

Church growth comes when we do not sit as a church body, taking resumés to weed out undesirables and attract the best possible candidates.

candlestick; and it giveth light unto all that are in the house. Let your light so shine before men, that they may see your good works, and glorify your Father which is in heaven." God didn't just save us so we can sit down and be satisfied with ourselves. Growing up in His purpose means understanding that God saved us for a reason.

THE SCAVENGER APPROACH (MISSIONS/SERVICE)

Growing up to His purpose means implementing His mandate to find them, bring them in, grow them up, and send them out. Church growth comes when we do not sit as a church body, taking resumés to weed out undesirables and attract the best possible candidates. One preacher called a local church in his area a "scavenger" church because they just took anybody. Well, I've got news for you: every church is supposed to be a scavenger church. We all ought to be just taking in anybody! We forget that, until God's grace cleaned us up and made us anew, we were all just an anybody. Every pastor and church member should be trying to give their church a bad reputation with the other local churches in their city. Your church ought to strive for the other churches to talk about you. The other churches in your city should be saying,

"Look at them! They took in that adulterer. They took in that crackhead. They took in that drunk. They took in that thief. They took in that child molester. They took in that gambler. They took in that murderer. Just look at them!"

Make the other churches indignant because your members overturn every rock in town to find the slimiest, the least and the lowest, and bring them to Jesus! Corporate executives can be just as sleazy and unsaved as a low-life junkie. In fact, the junkie may have more integrity than the sleazy executive because the junkie's sinful state is unhidden. Yet, most churches would be eager to have the corporate executive whose sleazy lifestyle is concealed, but not the junkie.

Church growth is out there, not inside the church walls. It's ours for the having; we have to go out there to get them. Scavengers don't sit back and wait for what they want. They go out looking. We need to go out looking for those who need Jesus. We have to train our members to not only give money for missions, but to give themselves, too.

Church growth is out there, not inside the church walls.

We are called to do, not just give money for others to go and do. The mission field has a calling for everyone in service to Him. But believers aren't just going to go out there. They have to be trained to know they're supposed to go. Christians must grow to understand that God expects His people to go where the people are, no matter where they are, and no matter who they are.

For church growth to happen, we shouldn't worry about who they are. Whether they are nobodies or somebodies is irrelevant.

We are all the same to Him. Some of us don't want to deal with the undesirable persons of this world on any level and aren't going to the corner to find any of them. In fact, we may even step over them on the way to church on Sunday morning so we can shout "hallelujah!" But to do this is *not* doing His will.

APPLICATION

What is the relationship between growing up to the Head in His purpose and church growth? First, churches that grow up to His purpose become "whosoever will" churches. Second, church members

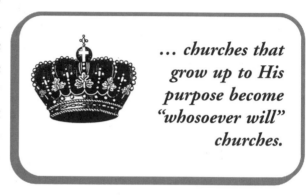

... churches that grow up to His purpose become "whosoever will" churches.

who have grown up in His purpose realize that they were chosen according to His divine knowledge and for His divine plan.

WHOSOEVER WILL CHURCHES

A church that has not made a commitment to bring in, "whosoever will" is going to be limited in its growth possibilities. If a church makes a decision that it doesn't want to grow, that's between that church and Jesus. And there are churches like that. They are often called "country club" churches. They only want their special group of friends and family to be there, occasionally letting in an acceptable candidate. Those churches don't grow, and it is clear that they don't want to grow. Churches who grow up in His purpose make a conscious decision to be a "whosoever will" church. That means the church finds them, brings them in, loves them and makes them feel at home.

Have you ever been invited to someone's home but still didn't quite feel welcome? The host may extend all the courtesies to you and be gracious, but you know that person really would rather not have you there. That's how some churches treat new believers. They *allow* them to be there and *tolerate* their presence. The person can't serve on any of the real "important" committees. They surely can't chair a standing committee. They may be allowed to serve on the usher board, but that's risky because they would be the first one to greet others. They may start making others like themselves feel welcome there, too. A church member who is serious about living for Jesus, won't remain at a church where he or she is merely tolerated. Sooner or later, they will head for a church where they can grow. When the purpose of the church is the same as God's purpose, all the people are accepted and challenged to grow.

> *When the purpose of the church is the same as God's purpose, all the people are accepted and challenged to grow.*

CHOSEN FOR A PURPOSE:
God Calls and Chooses According to His Divine Knowledge and Plan

Read a modern translation of Chapters 3 and 4 in the Book of Exodus. You may see in Moses a person who acted or looked like you when you stood in the presence of God and received His purpose for your life. You may have given God excuses when He revealed His purpose for you. Often, it is hard for us to accept the fact that the men and women of the Bible were just ordinary human beings whom God chose. Growing up in His purpose means accepting that God chooses us according to His divine knowledge—knowledge to which we are not privy. As we think on Bible personalities like Moses, we think of what he became, not how he began. Moses became more powerful as he grew in God's purpose for him and for Israel. God started Moses out with a simple act of changing a rod to a snake. Eventually, that rod guided the parting of the Red Sea.

Sometimes we think that when we fulfill God's purpose, everything will be easy and everyone else will go along with the plan. Rarely is it that easy. How wonderful it would be if everyone cooperated with God's plans! How simple it would have been if Pharaoh would have let the Israelites go when Moses told him the first time! Sometimes, when we are fulfilling God's purpose, we begin to wonder if we are really doing what God wants. Moses had to go to Pharaoh a total of twelve times before the Israelites were freed from bondage. This is important to remember in our own frustrations and stumbling blocks in fulfilling God's purpose. Just because we have to keep trying doesn't mean that God is not with us. Equally as important to remember is that God's purpose is ultimately fulfilled, no matter who tries to get in the way. If they try to get in the way too long, God will move them out of the way so that His will can be done. Growing up in His purpose means being willing to "keep on keeping on" in spite of obstacles.

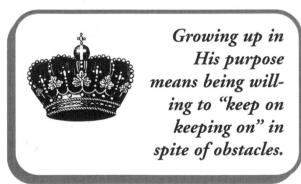

Growing up in His purpose means being willing to "keep on keeping on" in spite of obstacles.

An architect designs structures and makes plans for the completion of a building project. An architect makes designs according to what needs to be done. For instance, the twin towers of the World Trade Center in New York are designed to sway as much as three feet to accommodate the high winds. In California, many buildings along the San Andreas Fault are designed to shift so that there is flexibility of movement when an earthquake hits. To a person who knows nothing about building design, it would seem that a building should be as sturdy as possible, with no possibility of movement. But people who design buildings know better because of the knowledge they have gained through previous experience. Often, it seems to us humans that the plan God has should be different. But God knows better because He has infinite wisdom and knowledge.

God is our divine Architect, making plans to build up His highest creation according to what needs to be done.

God is our divine Architect, making plans to build up His highest creation according to what needs to be done. God has a place for each of us. He has a place or purpose for every one of His creatures. His design for us is perfect, but we, being human, do not carry out His purpose as He intended. When an architect designs a building, it is then left up to a number of other people to carry out the plan. Drafting technicians, builders, construction workers and artisans all share in the completion of the project. The importance of the other persons, beyond the architect, often does not become apparent until years later. You may know of a building or home that has serious structural problems because someone did not follow the architect's plan. Those flaws may not be evident until many years later, but it will become evident that someone did not complete his or her work properly. God's plan is without error. However, His plan is so great, even human error cannot cause it to go unful-filled. As we journey through life, we are in a constant state of fulfilling His plan, whether we are aware of it or not; whether we know its details or not.

Growing up to His purpose means trusting Him as the Architect of our faith journey.

After becoming a believer, a person may wonder, "Where does He want me to go? What does He want me to do?" The call or encounter was sure and clear, yet the manifestation is a little cloudy. Whenever our Lord calls us to a new thing, whether it's the first time or the tenth time, we have to trust that He has a purpose, even if we don't understand it at the time. Growing up to His purpose means trusting Him as the Architect of our faith journey. A call from God is always an opportunity to go on a new journey.

Growing up to His purpose may be a dangerous opportunity because, if we really yield ourselves to that growing process, we don't know where we'll end up. It happened to Abraham. It could happen to any of us. The Lord just told Abraham to go, but He didn't tell him where. Yet, Hebrews 11:8 praises Abraham as a model of faith because he was faithful to the Lord's calling. Growing up in His purpose is a dangerous opportunity if we are unable to trust Him. As the old folks sang, "Ain't no danger in God's waters." The only danger is losing ourselves in His purpose. If we lose ourselves to Him and His divine purpose, we gain eternal life, we grow up to

Him. A purpose-driven church is a growing church, and a purpose-driven Christian is a growing Christian.

Church members who have grown up to His purpose are willing to grow and be discipled. Those who truly become disciples become disciple-makers. Disciple-makers are constantly adding to the Kingdom, thus the body not only gets stronger, it gets bigger.

FOR STUDY AND REVIEW

Chapter Four
Growing Up to the Head in His Purpose

1. What is the five-fold purpose of the church?
   (a) _____
   (b) _____
   (c) _____
   (d) _____
   (e) _____

2. How has God revealed His purpose for your life? Does your understanding of your purpose evolve or do you understand it right away?

3. There is no difference between being religious and being a Christian.   True _____ or False _____.

4. What has God gifted you to do in fulfillment of His purpose? How does using (or not using) your gifts affect the growth of your church?

5. What is the three-fold purpose for every believer's gift? *(Ephesians 4:15)*

    a. _____

    b. _____

    c. _____

6. Match the following actions with the five-fold purpose of the church.

    Find   _____

    Bring   _____

    Grow   _____

    Send   _____

Growing Up in His Word

1. Re-read the Book of Ephesians, focusing on 3:1-14. Examine, identify and explain how God accomplished His eternal purpose through Jesus Christ.

2. Reflect on the following statement: "Growing up to His purpose may be a dangerous opportunity because, if we really yield ourselves to that growing process, we don't know where we'll end up." Think about the life of the Apostle Paul as it unfolds in the Book of Acts. How do you think the apostle would explain the above quote as it relates to his life?

Growing Up Together

Each church should have and use a mission statement to guide all activities of the church. Discuss how the mission statement of your church aligns with God's five-fold purpose for the church.

Growing Up to the Head!

What has God revealed to you as your purpose for existence? How are you fulfilling your God-given purpose? Does your individual purpose align with God's five-fold purpose for the church?

GROWING UP TO THE HEAD

In Prayer

T he Book of Ephesians is concerned with the perfecting of the church. That's why many scholars call Ephesians the "high watermark," the high peak in

For this cause I bow my knees unto the Father of our Lord Jesus Christ."

Ephesians 3:14

scriptural truth. Ephesians is about the church and, consequently, the people who make up the church.

Ephesians is, among other things, a book of intercessory prayer. Two great passages of prayer undergird and characterize this book. The first prayer is found in 1:15-23, and the second is found in 3:15-21. (See Essential #6, "Growing Up to the Head in His Love.") The second passage and other Scriptures will guide us in this chapter as we explore growing up in prayer.

A PRAYER FOR FULLNESS

Paul prays in verse 19 of the fourth chapter that the church might be filled with the fullness of God. A church and believer

Growing up in prayer means developing deep roots.

who are committed to spiritual growth will make Paul's prayer a portion of their own prayer. That way, they will grow up in prayer and in love. Growing up in prayer means developing deep roots. Paul's prayer was that the saints would be "rooted ..." so that "Christ may dwell in your hearts by faith, that ye, being rooted and grounded in love...."

A few years ago we had a severe snow storm in our area. After the storm I cut down all the pine trees in my front yard because one had fallen on my car and had just missed our home. I found out that pine trees, as beautiful and as tall as they are, don't have a good root system. They can be blown over as soon as a strong wind comes along, unlike the sequoia trees, of northern California, that have great root systems which make them grow so big and live so long. Not only do they have great root systems, but they spread their roots and tie in with other sequoia trees. So when the wind blows and storms come, they are anchored together in their roots. Paul prayed for the church to be anchored and rooted and grounded.

The Christian community could learn a great deal from the sequoia trees. When strong winds of tribulation try to knock us down, we should be able to draw upon the strength of one another. We should hold on to one another and strengthen each other. We need to be anchored in our roots and stick together like the sequoia trees.

We also need to be grounded. One of the things I know about construction is that good footing is needed. You've got to dig the footing deep in order to have a solid foundation. Once you have a solid foundation, you can make a few mistakes on the top. The roof may blow off but still you've got a

Being rooted and grounded means being anchored. It's good to be anchored.

house. Likewise, if the church and her membership are rooted and grounded in prayer, an occasional wrong decision will not leave the body devastated. It will survive.

Being rooted and grounded means being anchored. It's good to be anchored. If you're not anchored, when the wind blows, you might blow away. If you're not anchored, when the current gets a little swift, you might drift out to sea. If you're not anchored, even as a Christian, you may go back out into the world.

When we were in the Holy Land crossing the Suez Canal in our little boat, it seemed to me that the current was awfully swift. I was so glad that after we got across, the captain and his crew let down the anchor. I looked toward the back end of our little boat, and it was swaying with the current. Then I looked back at the other end that was anchored, and I knew that the boat could stay right there forever. At that moment new insight came to me concerning what it means for my soul to be anchored in the Lord.

Growing up in prayer means being anchored. It is good to be anchored. God's desire is for His children to be anchored. God wants the church anchored; so, He gave this word to Paul so that the church would be anchored in prayer. God wanted the church not only anchored, but rooted and grounded in the love of Christ.

CHRIST-CONSCIOUSNESS

I want to give two propositions relative to growing up in prayer. The first is the more we are conscious of Christ in us, the more we will let Christ live in us. In other words, the more we are conscious of Christ within us, the more we will walk and live in Him. Living in Him means, in part, growing up in prayer. Having a meaningful relationship with God, in many ways follows the same rule as having a meaningful relationship with another person. What does it take to have a meaningful relationship? What does it take to really get to know someone? It takes time. You can't know a person or have a meaningful relationship with a person unless you take time to spend with him or her.

The more time we spend in prayer, the more our love relationship with Him grows, and the more we grow up in Him.

After 36 years of marriage, I know my wife well, and she knows me. There are some things that people could tell me about my wife, Sadie, and I would be reasonably confident they are telling the truth because I know her nature. Likewise, there are some things people could tell me about her and I would know (inasmuch as is humanly possible) that they are wrong because I know her. I have spent many years getting to know her.

The same holds true if we wish to have a meaningful relationship with the Lord. We must spend time with Him. Spending time with the Lord means spending time in prayer. The more time we spend in prayer, the more our love relationship with Him grows, and the more we grow up in Him.

The second proposition is, the more we realize what Christ has done for us, the more we will desire to take the love and salvation of God to others. In the first essential, we addressed spiritual blessings. The more we spiritualize and internalize what Christ has done for us—or how He has blessed us—the more we will be likely to take the love of God and the salvation He offers through His Son to a dying, lost world.

If God has blessed you, you ought to tell somebody. If God has delivered you, you ought to tell somebody. If He's ever healed your body, you ought to tell somebody. And certainly, if you are saved from the penalty of sin, you ought to tell it. One of the twenty-three core values of the church where I pastor states, "We believe that every person deserves to hear a testimony about how good God has been to somebody else."

In summary, the more we pray, the more conscious we are of Christ in us. The more conscious we are of Christ in us, the more we will realize how much He has done for us, and we willingly share His goodness and His love. This will result in others being added to the church daily, which is what growing up to the head in prayer is all about.

A Prayer for the Church to Model

In the Bible, Paul's prayer in this passage is second only to the Lord's Prayer. This is a prayer for us to model. First and foremost, Paul prays for a specific cause. He says, "For this reason [or for this cause, for this purpose], I fall on my knees."

What was the purpose? What was the cause? It was for the great salvation and for the birth of the church. Paul loved the church. Paul was excited about its purpose.

When we pray, it is good to get on our knees. It's not a physical thing. It's a submission thing; it's a humility thing; it's a surrender thing. When we get down on our knees in front of somebody, it's an act of submission or humility. It means we're turning it over, we're surrendering, we're getting out of fighting position altogether. It's not the actual act of getting on our knees that counts. What's important is what it symbolizes.

It's just like when we praise God. When we lift our hands, it's not a physical thing, but an adoration thing. Lifting our hands in praise is also a surrender thing. It's no more than what you would do if someone came up behind you and put their finger in your back and said "stick 'em up." What would you do? That's all God is saying: "stick 'em up." It is not a physical thing. It's a surrender thing.

Paul says for this cause, "I am so thankful that I fall down on my knees and I pray that the church would be anchored in prayer and rooted and grounded in love." He is not talking about just the church at Ephesus, and he's certainly not talking about just the stained-glass windows. He's talking about each and every saint. He's talking about us. The prayer is for you and me. It is also my prayer that every believer be anchored in prayer and rooted and grounded in *agape* (unconditional love).

> *Growing up in prayer means learning to pray the way God teaches us to pray through the study of His word.*

KNOWING HOW TO PRAY

Growing up in prayer means learning to pray the way God teaches us to pray through the study of His word. Growing up in prayer is praying with authority and power. Growing up in prayer is praying in accordance with the Word of God and based on the promises of God. Growing up in prayer means praying as God teaches us to pray—and no other way.

Paul's prayer for the church at Ephesus teaches us about intercessory

> *... knowing how to pray means understanding that in the flesh we never really know how to pray nor what we should pray.*

prayer. But what about when we pray for ourselves? Jesus teaches that when we pray for ourselves, we are to "enter in to thy closet, and when thou hast shut thy door, pray to thy Father which is in secret; and thy Father which seeth in secret shall reward thee openly" (Matthew 6:6). I am so glad that God not only hears my prayers, but if I pray as He has taught me, He sees and rewards me openly.

When He sees me crying, He wipes away my tears. When he sees me burdened down, He lifts me up. When He sees me hurting, He soothes my pain. He sees me weak, and He strengthens me.

Believers who have grown up to the Head in prayer realize that when they pray as God has taught them, God not only hears their prayer, but sees their condition as well. Also, knowing how to pray means understanding that in the flesh we never really know how to pray nor what we should pray.

Romans 8:26-27 teaches, "Likewise the Spirit also helpeth our infirmities: for we know not what we should pray for as we ought: but the Spirit itself maketh intercession for us with groanings which cannot be uttered. And he that searcheth the hearts knoweth what is the mind of the Spirit, because he maketh intercession for the saints according to the will of God."

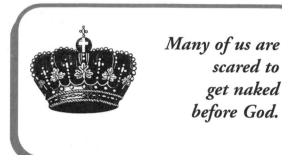

Many of us are scared to get naked before God.

We must be a prepared, available vessel. I believe that is why God asks us to go into the closet and close the door. When we close the door, we can get naked before Him and take off all our humanness, all our restraints, all our doubts, all our pride and confess all our sins. Many of us are scared to get naked before God. However, we must remember, He will not see anything He has not seen before. He is the one who birthed us. He is the One who changed our diapers. God, in fact, already sees our most naked and vulnerable state. The act of humbling ourselves, of revealing ourselves fully to Him, guides us to growing up in prayer. It is our willingness, our desire, which touches the heart of God. When we pray as God teaches us to pray, we must humble ourselves before Him.

Becoming a prepared vessel not only means positioning ourselves properly, but also means getting into the right relationship with Him. Believers who have grown up in prayer realize that praying as God taught us to pray depends on a right relationship. Philippians 2:5 tells us, "Let this mind be in you, which was also in Christ Jesus." Romans 12:2 tells us, "Be not conformed to this world: but be ye transformed by the renewing of your mind, that ye may prove what is that good, and acceptable, and perfect, will of God."

The key to praying as God teaches us is knowing the will of God. In order to know the will of God we must have the mind of Christ. For indeed God has stated, "And this is the confidence that we have in him, that, if we ask any thing according to his will, he heareth us." (1 John 5:14). Therefore, praying in right relationship with Him means being of His mind by the transforming power of the Holy Spirit. When we pray in the knowledge of His will and are confident that

> *...praying in right relationship with Him means being of His mind by the transforming power of the Holy Spirit.*

we are asking according to His will, we have the assurance that He will hear our prayer.

Not only must our position and our relationship with God be right, we must also have the right motives. Jesus warns us to pray not like the hypocrites or the heathen. Matthew 6:5, 7, 8 states:

> "And when thou prayest, thou shalt be not be as the hypocrites are: for they love to pray standing in the synagogues and in the corners of the streets, that they may be seen of men. Verily I say unto you, They have their reward.... But when ye pray, use not vain repetitions, as the heathen do: for they think that they shall be heard for their much speaking. Be not ye therefore like unto them: for your Father knoweth what things ye have need of, before ye ask him."

Remember, the Father sees our motives. It is not necessary to pray loudly, repetitively, or eloquently, for God knows what we need even before we ask Him. Growing up in prayer means praying in the right position, with the right relationship and the right motives.

KNOWING WHAT TO PRAY FOR

There are six petitions in Paul's prayer to the church at Ephesus. The first one is for strength and power for the inner being, for within. Secondly, he prays for Christ to rule and reign within. The third petition is for love that is rooted and grounded within. Verse eighteen contains the fourth request, which is for understanding of spiritual truth. Request five is to know the love of God (verse nineteen). And the sixth petition is for the fullness of God.

Notice something: every petition is for something internal, for the inner being. Nowhere in this prayer does he pray for a car. Nowhere in this prayer does he pray for a good job. Those are acceptable prayer requests, but they are not found in this prayer. Nowhere in this prayer is anybody praying for a wife or a husband. Nowhere in this prayer is anybody even praying for a blessing of physical healing. There is nothing external about this prayer. The prayer is for the inner being to be strengthened. Paul's prayer is for the inner self to have an indwelling of God.

It is possible for God to live in you but not be at home in you.

You might say that God lives in all saints. While He does live in all saints, He's not at home in all saints. It is possible for God to live in you but not be at home in you. In some of us, God doesn't know what bed He's going to sleep in from one night to another. You might even put Him out of the bed. Sometimes He may get fed; at other times He may not. Maybe He doesn't know what time the door locks because there is no discipline in the heart. This prayer is for the inner self to be strengthened and that God may feel at home and comfortable in your heart. This prayer is for the inner being to have an understanding of spiritual things, and the inner self to experience the fullness of God.

THE INNER BEING VS. OUTER NEEDS

The Church is the body of Christ, and Christ is the Head. The Church has a perfect Head. The body, however, has not grown up proportionately to the Head. Paul's prayer is for balance, for the fullness of the presence of God within the life of the person and of the Church.

There is a clear spiritual ad-monition—that in the mind of Christ, He feels incomplete until the body is full. I don't quite understand that,

Growing up in prayer means giving less attention to the external things and more attention to the self within.

knowing how complete God is. But in His own mind He feels incomplete. This is His prayer for the church: that we have the fullness of the presence of Christ.

Two problems can be identified. The first is that we never pray for our inner being because external needs tend to consume us. Have you prayed recently for your inner being? Growing up in prayer means giving less attention to the external things and more attention to the self within. In Matthew 6:25-34, Jesus admonishes us not to focus on the external things but to seek first God's kingdom and God's righteousness. Those things will come because God knows what we need, and He desires to meet those needs.

But on the other hand, there's another you, the outer you. The outer you may need a new car; the outer you may need a

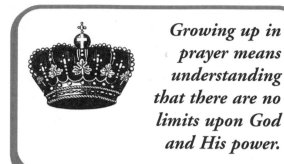

Growing up in prayer means understanding that there are no limits upon God and His power.

job; the outer you needs companionship. These are the types of things we pray for concerning the external being. Growing up in prayer means having prayer in the proper perspective. It means having the assurance that God knows what we need and will take care of our needs. Growing up in prayer requires praying for change to come from within. Have you prayed for your inner being that you might be strengthened? Have you prayed that you might understand all spiritual knowledge and understand the love that surpasses knowledge? Has it been your desire that the inner person be anchored, rooted and grounded in the love of Christ? Many of us have missed that in our prayers. We pray for a lot of stuff, but we forget to pray for the inner being, the inner person. That means we have not fully grown up in prayer. When we pray for our inner being, it is a sign of greater spiritual maturity because that is where true change occurs, not on the outside.

The second problem we face is that we box God into our own limitations. Even in our prayers and thoughts, we sometimes feel a limitation according to what we think is going to happen, or according to what someone else has said is going to happen. In this process, somehow we box God in, not knowing that God is able to do anything. What's impossible to humans is possible to God. Too often, we lock Him to our own imagination, our own limitations. Growing up in prayer means understanding that there are no limits upon God and His power.

Growing up in prayer means realizing you cannot estimate prayer power. You can estimate how much dynamite it will take to blow up a building. You can estimate how long it will take you to drive a certain distance. A meteorologist can estimate the power or potency of a hurricane and its expected time of arrival. But you cannot estimate prayer power. Prayer power is controlled and limited only by God, and *God has no limits.*

A Prayer for Love

Paul's prayer is that we be rooted and grounded in love. He describes the love in geometric terms. He refers to it as the height and depth. He talks about it being wide and long, deep and high. Paul says His love is so wide that His arms can envelope the whole world with love. So wide that He can reach those who think they're out of reach or who think they have drifted so far they are anchorless—those who have been out in the world and have backslidden too far. We even try to limit God's ability to forgive by holding on to past sins and memories of how we used to be.

Not only is His love wide, but His love is long. How long? From here to eternity, that's how long. But really, from eternity to eternity because God is eternal. That's how long God's love is. How long? So long that while we were yet sinners, He commended His Son to die on the cross for us. He commended His Son while we were yet whoremongers…while we were yet drinking liquor…while we were yet snorting stuff up our noses…while we were yet fornicating and adulterating and idolizing. While we were yet sinners, His love was so long that before we even got saved, He predestined and made provision for our salvation–that's how long.

The text also says that His love is deep and His love is high. His love is deep enough to go from riches to rags ... deep enough to think it not robbery that He would step down from His throne into earth and heal and minister and teach, and then to die on an old rugged cross where His blood was spilled. That's how deep. His love is high enough to reach the tallest mountain as well as deep enough to flow to the lowest valley.

The Psalmist tells us in Psalm 139:11:

> "If I say surely darkness will cover me, even the night shall be light about me. Yea, the darkness hideth not from thee; but the night shineth as the day: the darkness and the light are both alike to thee."

AN OLD TESTAMENT INTERCESSORY MODEL PRAYER (ISAIAH 62:5-8)

God appointed 167 watchmen on the walls of Zion to make intercessory prayer for the establishment of God's kingdom on earth and for the glory of Jerusalem. New Testament believers can learn a lot about growing up to the Head in intercessory prayer from this model. The watchmen prayed non-stop. They took turns and prayed all day and all night. Think about the spiritual and numerical growth of a church if members were watching and praying over the church all day and all night. I am reminded of the words of a song the old church used to sing: "All night, all day, angels watching over me, my Lord." The watchmen watched and prayed. Jesus asked the disciples in the Garden of Gethsemane to watch and pray. Those who watched and prayed put arms and legs on their prayers.

The story is told of one who was being victimized by a rising tide. The flood had come upon his homeland, and the young man attempted to flee by first going to the upper level of his home.

Later he ascended to the roof; still later he went to the highest point of the chimney, as the flood waters continued to rise. As the story goes, someone came by in a canoe

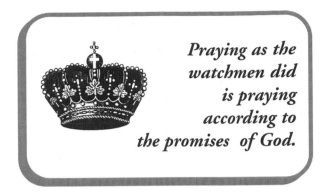

Praying as the watchmen did is praying according to the promises of God.

to save him. The man refused the offer of a canoe ride, indicating that he would wait for the Lord to come and save him. Later a helicopter flew by and dropped a rope and ladder, inviting the man to come aboard. Again he declined, indicating that he would wait there for the Lord to save him. Eventually the man drowned and was taken up to heaven. At the Pearly Gates, he complained to St. Peter about the Lord not saving him. St. Peter replied, "God sent you a canoe, a rope and a ladder, and you refused all three. What more did you want Him to do to try and save you?"

The moral of the story is that we need to put arms and legs on our prayers. If you are praying about a certain situation, don't just sit and pray—watch and pray. This means that you don't just pray, you put action to your prayers.

Remember, God loves to help those who are willing to work along side Him to help themselves. The watchmen prayed without ceasing. We, like the watchmen, must cry out to God and "give Him no rest" until He brings to fruition what He has promised. Notice that they did this by reminding God and the people about the promises of God. He certainly doesn't need reminding about His promises; however, God enjoys our relationship with Him by knowing that we know His promises. Praying as the watchmen did is praying according to the promises of God.

God's promise was that He would provide protection. So they prayed in Isaiah 62:8, "The Lord hath sworn by his right hand, and by the arm of his strength, Surely I will no more give thy corn to be meat for thine enemies; and the sons of the stranger shall not drink thy wine, for that which thou has laboured."

They also prayed for provision, and God promised that He would provide. So they prayed as in Isaiah 62:9, "But they that have gathered it shall eat it, and praise the Lord; and they that have brought it together shall drink it in the courts of my holiness." The remainder of the watchmen's prayer was spent in praise. If we, like the watchmen, will make intercessory prayer for the church without ceasing, according to the promises of God, He will bless our churches tremendously. God has promised that one day the church—the bride, perfect and all grown up—will be presented to Christ, the Groom (Ephesians 5:27).

Praying as the watchmen prayed on the wall of Zion is what I call praying on higher ground. Johnson Oatman, Jr. penned it well in the song, "Higher Ground":

> "Still praying as I onward bound,
> Lord, plant my feet on higher ground.
> My heart has no desire to stay,
> Where doubts arise and fears dismay.
> Though some may dwell, Where some abound,
> My prayer, my aim is higher ground."

Growing up in prayer means learning to pray on higher ground.

Earlier I mentioned that Paul's prayer to the church at Ephesus is second only to the Lord's Prayer. It is important to realize that Paul, like the watchmen, ends this prayer in praise, in a doxology. For the last eighteen years I have devoted myself to teaching and preaching that praise is a part of prayer and

prayer is a part of
praise. You can't real-
ly pray a prayer to
God without prais-
ing God. Some of us
are praying but
there is no praise in
the prayer. Growing
up in prayer means

*Growing up in
prayer means
knowing that
we must praise
when we pray.*

knowing that we must praise when we pray. Growing up, or
maturing, means that we praise and pray even when we don't
feel like we've got much to praise for.

Even in Jesus' model prayer, He opened and closed it in praise.
The first four lines are all praise: "Hallowed be thy name, Thy
kingdom come, Thy will be done ..." He praised God before He
said, "Give me this day my daily bread, Lead me ..." Then Jesus
closed it with, "Thy kingdom come, thy will be done ... forever ..."

In verses twenty and twenty-one of the Ephesians passage,
God has Paul close this prayer in praise. Paul says, "Now unto
him that is able to do exceeding abundantly above all that we ask
or think, according to the power that worketh in us, Unto him
be glory in the church by Christ Jesus throughout all ages, world
without end. Amen."

GOD IS ABLE

Growing up in prayer means knowing that God is able,
despite the circumstance, despite how impossible the situation looks. The purpose of answered prayer is that God might
have the glory in the church through Jesus Christ. If you have
received an answer to your prayer, you ought to give Him the
glory. Has He delivered you? You ought to give Him the glory.

The reason God answered your prayer is so you can praise Him and say, "Glory be to God!"

God is able. The devil doesn't want you to know about the ableness of God.

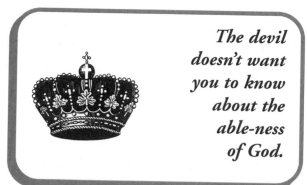

The devil doesn't want you to know about the able-ness of God.

According to the Scripture, He's able to do things exceeding, abundantly, above all that we can ask, think, or even imagine. He's able to take a little boy's lunch and feed 5,000 hungry people. He's able to pull a dead man, Lazarus, out of a grave. He's able to take a woman who has a lifelong hemorrhage and heal her. What God has done for these is no more than He can do for you. He's able! He's able! He's able! He's able to do it according to the power that works in the inner being. That's why it is so important to grow up in prayer.

A believer who has grown up to the Head in prayer knows it is not the outer condition that he or she needs to be concerned about. It is the inner being that is most important. The inner being is who we really are. God works through the inner being. He's able to do it according to the power that worketh in us. To Him be the glory in the church through Jesus Christ our Lord and Savior, through all ages, forever.

APPLICATION

How does growing up in prayer relate to building God's kingdom and to the growth of the church? The believer who has grown up in prayer will evidence this in a number of ways.

First, in his or her personal life, the believer will not get caught up in praying primarily for temporal things. A believer who has grown up in prayer is concerned about

A believer who has grown up in prayer is concerned about change from within.

change from within. Such a believer knows that "our battle is not against flesh and blood but against the powers, principalities and rulers of this world."

Second, believers who have grown up to the Head will give evidence of not just praying, but praying in faith. Praying in faith means praying according to God's will and then believing he will answer that prayer. Praying in faith involves behaving as though God has already done what you're asking for in prayer. If the believer has prayed in faith that God will bless the church with growth, the believer then acts like he or she already belongs to a growing church. There is a high expectation and anticipation relative to growth. Evangelistic efforts will increase because arms and legs are always a part of prayers that are prayed in faith. The invitation or decision time at the close of the sermon becomes a time of great excitement.

Third, a believer who has grown up to the Head in prayer knows how to praise God. In His prayers, Jesus first offered words of praise to God before pouring out words of petition. Grown up prayer recognizes and praises God's power and ability, no matter what the outcome. Growing up in prayer means stating confidently, as did Shadrach, Meshach and Abednego, "We know God is able, but even if He does not, we will not bow down." The mature believer understands the "even if He does

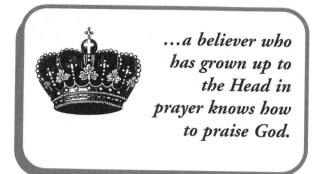

...a believer who has grown up to the Head in prayer knows how to praise God.

not" part of his or her reply to the King. Those three young men would not serve another god even if their God chose *not* to deliver them. That is the difficult part for most believers. It is often difficult for us to understand why God has not done what we know He is able to do. In these instances, more often than not, we end up praising God for not answering the prayer in the way that we had originally hoped.

A church comprised of believers who have grown up in prayer will pray that the will of God be done in their church. That means supporting decisions that are prayerfully made by the church, even if you didn't vote in favor of it.

Fourth, a believer who has grown up to the Head in prayer will know and demonstrate the difference between intercessory prayer and personal prayer. The church will benefit from this because the church will not be victimized by selfish prayer in collective worship. According to what we have learned about praying as God has taught us to pray, collective worship demands 100 percent intercessory prayer. Intercessory prayer based on the promises of God is what is needed for church growth. Believers who have matured in their prayer life will constantly make intercession for the life of the church. They may even lead or join a ministry of intercessory prayer that has as its main function to undergird the church and the pastor in prayer.

Fifth, the believer who has grown up to the Head in prayer has constantly been in the presence of God. Believers that are constantly in the presence of God experience less anxiety than those who are rarely in His presence. Mature, less anxious Christians attract the presence of others—those desiring to know the Source of their peace. Immature,

Prayer is the solution and alternative to worry. You cannot pray and worry at the same time.

anxious Christians drive others from their presence. God has not promised that believers will be immune from suffering, trials and tribulations. But He told us we should not be anxious. His Word tells us, "And why take ye thought for raiment? Consider the lilies of the field, how they grow; they toil not, neither do they spin" (Matthew 6:28). Church members who have grown up in prayer don't exhibit a lot of worry and turmoil in their lives because they have learned to trust.

Prayer is the solution and alternative to worry. You cannot pray and worry at the same time. Prayer and worry are incompatible. Believers who have reached a point of spiritual maturity not only understand this principle, but they also apply it to their daily lives. Therefore, people are attracted to them and the church. Worry-free believers help create a mess-free environment. A worry-free, mess-free environment can only enhance church growth. An anxious environment creates tension and hinders church growth.

In summary, those who have been in His presence are filled with His presence, and those who are filled with His presence will attract others to His presence. Apply this principle to your life and to the life of your church, and church growth will be evident.

Sixth, growing up in prayer means living in the fullness of His love. Have you ever thought about how much God must love

... growing up in prayer means wanting to tell others what He has done for you.

you? I'm not talking about how much God loves His creation, humanity. I'm talking about knowing how much God loves you, all by yourself. That's living in His fullness because we know that all He has is ours. When you are aware of His fullness, you are in a greater position to love others, to show *agape* toward all of humanity. You can make the effort to love others unconditionally because you are loved unconditionally by God. It means you are less likely to be judgmental toward others because you are able to love. A judgmental Christian stifles church growth. A non-judgmental Christian enhances the life and growth of the church.

Seventh, growing up in prayer means wanting to tell others what He has done for you. It's like you're really itching to tell somebody. It's a good idea to keep a prayer journal. After some time has passed, go back and look at some of your prayer requests. Go back and praise God for the things He has done. When you go back and look at those requests and see how good God has been to you, it makes you want to tell somebody. You can't keep it to yourself!

A believer who has grown up to the Head in prayer knows that God's deliverance did not come simply for that believer's joy and ful-

God delivers us to bring glory unto Himself.

Growing up in prayer means giving God the glory and not being ashamed.

fillment. God delivers us to bring glory unto Himself. Growing up in prayer means giving God the glory and not being ashamed. It is very easy for us to become confused about this. When we look over our lives and see our jobs, families, homes, cars, health and the like, our thoughts and conversations can ever so quickly and easily turn to what "I" did, leaving God out altogether. Growing up in prayer means giving God the glory for everyday things in our everyday conversations.

In summary, a believer whose personal life reflects being grown up in prayer is a transformed, contagious church member. One who is contagious attracts by giving. One who is contagious lures others simply by being who he or she is. A contagious Christian is a contagious witness. A contagious Christian inspires others to want to go out, do good and tell the Good News.

For Study and Review

Chapter Five
Growing Up to the Head in Prayer

1. Ephesians is, among other things, a book of _____ prayer.

2. The two great passages of prayer that undergird and characterize the Book of Ephesians are _____ and _____.

3. How has (can) growing up in prayer helped you to develop so that you may weather the strong winds of tribulation?

4. What are the two propositions relative to growing up in prayer discussed in this chapter?

5. What is the church's responsibility concerning prayer?

6. In order to grow up to the Head in prayer, it is critical that we know how to pray. The author lists five conditions which should be included in every believer's prayer. List them below.

7. What does it mean to become a prepared vessel?

8. List the six petitions in Paul's prayer to the church of Ephesus.

    (a) _____

    (b) _____

    (c) _____

    (d) _____

    (e) _____

    (f) _____

Growing Up in His Word

1. Read the Book of Ephesians, focusing on Ephesians 3:14-21. To kneel before someone is an act of submission and humility. It also recognizes one with authority greater than oneself. What were the petitions Paul requested of the Lord? Who would benefit from the Lord's granting the requests? *(Think about it ...)* What were some possible results of God granting Paul's requests?

Growing Up Together

The author lists five ways which will be evidenced by a believer and church that has grown up to the Head in prayer. List those five conditions and discuss how each has impacted your church by its presence or absence.

(1)

(2)

(3)

(4)

(5)

Growing Up to the Head!

Are you a contagious church member? Does your life attract others? What are some transformations that have taken place in your life that you know only could have happened through prayer? What areas of your life, if any, have you identified as still needing the transforming power of prayer?

GROWING UP TO THE HEAD

In His Love

Paul's vision for the church and the people was for them to be anchored in prayer and rooted and grounded in love. He wanted this so they would know the love of Christ.

And to know the love of Christ, which passeth knowledge, that ye might be filled with all the fullness of God. **Ephesians 3:19**

Growing up to the Head in His love means experiencing His love. This love, he says, surpasses knowledge, the head stuff. Our own head, with the little "h," can get us into a lot of trouble. Paul wants us to experience something greater than the head with the little "h" can ever fully comprehend. Knowledge comes from the head; love comes from the Heart, and this is what Paul is addressing in the passage.

Sometimes it seems like it should be unnecessary to explain what Paul was talking about when he mentioned love. In my years of pastoring, I've found that it is indeed necessary because people sometimes fail to remember that there are different types

Human beings cannot be sustained on a type of love that simply "turns them on."

of love. Paul was talking about *agape*. In the Greek language there are three words for love.

Eros is the Greek word that describes passionate physical love or sexual love. I am never so aware of how *eros* "ain't nothing but a thang" then when I talk to couples involved in teenage pregnancy. Back in my day, which some may call antiquated, when a young girl got pregnant, there was either a shotgun wedding or there was going to be some hard discussion about marriage. But today, many times, marriage is not even a consideration. With the honesty God gave them, both males and females alike come into my office and say, "It wasn't nothing. We just made love. No, we don't want to get married. I don't like him/her. We just did it."

Often, young people, and some older men and women, fail to realize that *eros* is shallow and fleeting. Romantic love and/or sexual love, even in the best of marriages, does not remain constant. Therefore, those who unite solely for the sake of *eros* are destined for disappointment. The joy of *eros* is short-lived. *Eros* does not compare to *agape*. Human beings cannot be sustained on a type of love that simply "turns them on."

Another type of love recognized is *philos*. It is the Greek root word used in the name of the city of Philadelphia, the city of brotherly love. Brotherly love is the type of love that can be understood as mutual love. *Philos* involves two people, not necessarily romantically involved, caring for and loving each other. But Jesus reminds us in Matthew 5:46 that we're not doing anything all that great by demonstrating *philos:* "For if ye love them which love you, what reward have ye? do not even the publicans the same?" It is easy for us to maintain loving feelings toward someone who loves us in return.

> *Agape doesn't depend on human feelings because it is rooted in something which is beyond human understanding.*

In Ephesians Chapter 3, Paul, under God's inspiration, is talking about being rooted and grounded in *agape*. This kind of love is usually translated as "unconditional love." It is the kind of love that keeps on loving, no matter what the beloved does. *Agape* is vastly different from *eros* and *philos*. The latter two are somewhat dependent upon mutual feelings. It's possible to desire someone who doesn't want you, but it's so much better when it's mutual. It's possible to care about someone who doesn't care about you, but it's so much better when he or she does. There is nothing wrong with having *eros* or *philos*. But neither can fill the soul because they are rooted in human feelings.

Agape does not depend on human feelings because it is rooted in something which is beyond human understanding. Unconditional love, *agape*, can only come from God. It is not possible for human beings in the flesh to know *agape*. It goes against the human instinct to love someone no matter what. That's the kind of love Paul is referring to in Romans Chapter 8, when he said, "Who shall separate us from the love of Christ? shall tribulation, or distress, or persecution, or famine, or nakedness, or peril, or sword?

"Nay, in all these things we are more than conquerors through him that loved us. For I am persuaded, that neither death, nor life, nor angels, nor principalities, nor powers, nor things present, nor things to come, Nor height, nor depth, nor any other creature, shall be able to separate us from the love of God, which is in Christ Jesus our Lord" (Romans 8:37-39).

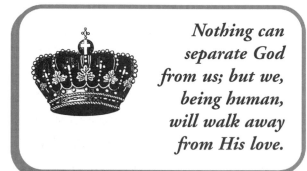

Nothing can separate God from us; but we, being human, will walk away from His love.

Now if you read that passage right, it means nothing can separate God's love *from us*. Don't ever read that and think that nothing can separate your love from God because you can fall out of love with God so quickly. Nothing can separate God from us; but we, being human, will walk away from His love. If you don't believe me, just ask Peter. Poor Peter was totally committed in Matthew 26:31. By the end of that chapter, he was weeping because he had denied even knowing Jesus. Still, Jesus kept loving him. The Lord knew Peter was merely human and had not yet grown up. Even though Peter was the only one to deny knowing Jesus verbally, all the disciples ran away because they were afraid. After His resurrection, however, Christ called all of His disciples back together. He loved them more than they understood. Nothing can separate God's love from us.

Even though we were created by a perfect God, we are pretty fickle. As Christians we claim to love Him, but there are times when another person would never know it. We treat God like a somebody who's in love with someone who's not very attractive. Have you ever known someone like that? A woman may marry a man who's really good to her. He compliments, encourages and comforts her. He gives her money to go shopping. He works hard and doesn't run around with other women. Yet, she's ashamed to take him out in public because of his physical appearance. She may take him around her family members, but she's still ashamed of the way he looks. She enjoys the benefits of the relationship, yet she will not acknowledge him publicly. Instead of her proudly parading this good man, she's ashamed because she's worried about what other people might think about the way he looks. That's immaturity. A person, no matter how old, whose love only goes that far has not grown up in His love.

Some Christians treat God like that. They go to church and pray and praise. But when they get away from church folk, they act like they don't know Him. We are scared that folks are going to laugh at us or call us religious fanatics. It is easy to

... many Christians go undercover between Sundays.

testify in the church. The majority of the people in the church know and love Jesus. But when you go to work in the morning, the majority of the people you meet may or may not know and love Jesus. Somebody may laugh at you when you stand up for Jesus. Somebody may make fun of you when you tell them that you are a Christian. Therefore, many Christians go undercover between Sundays. We have an undercover religion. Growing up in His love means not being ashamed of the One you love.

I knew a couple in their late sixties who seemed to really enjoy their married life. One day the wife explained to me that this was a second marriage for them both. He had been widowed, and she had divorced a man who was very abusive toward her. Her second husband was very loving, patient and kind. One day she told him, "You know, I never would have married you when I was young because you can't dance." In her youthful immaturity, she would have been ashamed to marry a good man simply because he couldn't dance. That was important to her in her twenties. Forty years later, she had matured to understand what really mattered in a love relationship. Growing up to the Head in His love means understanding what is really important in a love relationship.

Theoretically, there are two basic types of loving relationships that human beings have. The first type is platonic relationships. In a platonic relationship, you just love the person like a friend—no strings, just love. Now, that sounds good. It sounds close to the Christian understanding of *agape*. Don't get it confused, however. Human beings also have monogamous relationships. That comes from the root word "mono," meaning "one." In other words, you have one love. When my wife and I first got married 36 years ago, we decided that we were not going to have a platonic type of marriage relationship. We vowed to have a monogamous relationship. In the family of God, God must be first, spouse second, and mama and daddy and everybody else have to take a number. That's monogamy. Some of us are dealing platonically with God. And, just like some people pollute the marital relationship with other adulterous relationships, people will allow other people and other things to pollute their relationship with God.

If you really love Jesus, you will readily give yourself to what God is calling for: a monogamous relationship. Some of us want Him to be our Friend, but we don't want him to be our Father. Some of us want Him as our Savior, but we don't

> *If you really love Jesus, you will readily give yourself to what God is calling for: a monogamous relationship*

want Him as our Lord. Some of us want to call on Him today, but we don't want to call on Him everyday. We want to be His friend, but we don't want to be His lover. But God is saying, "Step over into a monogamous relationship with Me."

If you decide you want a monogamous relationship with Him, the first thing you must do is choose Him. We have to make a choice to love God with all our heart, with all our soul, with all our might and to have no other god(s) before Him. "Hear, O Israel: The LORD our God is one LORD: And thou shalt love the LORD thy God with all thine heart, and with all thy soul, and with all thy might" (Deuteronomy 6:4-5). These verses are a part of what is known as the *Shema*. When asked about the "greatest commandment," Jesus answered by quoting the *Shema* (Mark 12:29). That means before we can get to the Great Commission, we've got to understand the *Shema*. We've got to love God more than we love the opinions of our friends if we should go out witnessing. We've got to love God more than we love the comfort of our bed on Sunday morning when it is time for Sunday School. We must love God more than we love the expensive clothes we buy instead of paying our tithe. We've got to love God more than anything! Growing up in His love means that pleasing God is more important to us

> *Growing up in His love means that pleasing God is more important to us than pleasing others.*

than pleasing others. Growing up in His love includes understanding that we must love God above everything and everyone.

Growing up to the Head in His love means choosing Him. Serving God is a choice. Being monogamous to Him is a choice. In Joshua 24:15, he told the people, "And if it seem evil unto you to serve the LORD, choose you this day whom ye will serve; whether the gods which your fathers served that were on the other side of the flood, or the gods of the Amorites, in whose land ye dwell: but as for me and my house, we will serve the LORD." At the time he made that statement, Joshua was an old man. He had seen the hand of God working in his life as well as the lives of the other Israelites.

An elderly Joshua had grown weary of the people's foolishness concerning God. He reminded them of how good and faithful God had been to them and their ancestors. He then reminded them of how wicked and polygamous their ancestors had been. Joshua told them, "Now, realizing this, you can do whatever you like. But as for me and my house, we are going to serve Yahweh." There were other gods being served, but Joshua wanted to be true to the one true God who had been true to them. Joshua wanted monogamy with God for him and his household.

What Joshua said to the Israelites is still true today. Many of us have seen the hand of God working among our people, within our families and in our own lives. Still, we are wishy-washy about taking a firm stand to serve Him. We can even recall a legion of blessings that He has bestowed upon us, yet remain tight-lipped before the world.

LOVE IN ACTION

When the resurrected Savior appeared to His disciples in the Book of John, He posed a question to Peter: "Jesus saith to Simon Peter, Simon, son of Jonah, lovest thou me more than these? He saith unto him, Yea, Lord; thou knowest that I love thee. He saith unto him, Feed my lambs. He saith to him again the second time, Simon, son of Jonas, lovest thou me? He saith unto him, Yea, Lord; thou knowest that I love thee. He saith unto him, Feed my sheep. He saith unto him the third time, Simon, son of Jonas, lovest thou me? Peter was grieved because he said unto him the third time, Lovest thou me? And he said unto him, Lord, thou knowest all things; thou knowest that I love thee. Jesus saith unto him, Feed my sheep" (John 21:15-17).

It is understandable that Peter was upset that the Savior kept questioning his love. But the limitations of the English word for love do not reveal the deeper meaning of the dialog between Peter and the Savior. The risen Lord was asking for one type of love and Peter was giving Him another. We defined the three primary Greek terms for love earlier in this chapter. Keeping those in mind, the conversation between Jesus and Peter could have gone something like this:

Jesus: Peter, do you *agape* me?
Peter: Yes, Lord. I *philos* you.
Jesus: Then feed my lambs.
Jesus: Peter, do you *agape* me?
Peter: Yes, Lord. I *philos* you.
Jesus: Then feed my sheep.

Then Jesus gave Peter a third opportunity to explain His love. But this time, Jesus used Peter's term for love.

Jesus: Peter, do you really even have *philos* for me?

Jesus was asking if Peter loved Him unconditionally with the type of love that would place no other before Him. Peter responded that he loved Jesus like a brother or a friend. Jesus then questioned whether Peter loved Him as a friend. In all of Jesus' responses to Peter's answers, He gave Peter a charge: "Feed my lambs/sheep." Perhaps Jesus changed His question about love to be on a level that Peter could understand. Still, no matter how deep (or how shallow) Peter's love for the Savior, he was still charged to take care of His people. Love for God translates into action. Growing up to the Head in His love means taking action for His sake.

Growing up in His love teaches us that love is more than a feeling.

Sometimes our actions are not consistent with our words in the Christian community. We want to say loving words without doing loving deeds. There is a saying, "Put your money where your mouth is." The world is calling upon the Christian community to "put your love where your mouth is." Growing up in His love means giving. Godly love, *agape*, often involves sacrifice. It involves risk. It involves extending ourselves beyond human limitations because the love is divinely inspired.

Love is not a feeling. Growing up in His love teaches us that love is more than a feeling. Love is always an act of giving, in one form or another. Because of His love, God has given each of us gifts, that we might share them with one another and with those who do not know Him. If we do not share God's love through our gifts, they are useless. If we fail to extend ourselves in Christian love by sharing our spiritual gifts, we paralyze those gifts. They are there, but there is no movement in them.

SHARING OUR GIFTS

We (the church) are not using all that God has given us. We want to hoard our gifts and not share them in love. God so loved the world that He gave His only begotten Son. He loves us enough to give us gifts and talents. Surely we can love enough to give those talents in His service. The problem with giving is that we want to lay hold to our spiritual gifts and use them as we want, not as He wants. The problem with giving of that which God has given us is that God does not allow us to discriminate. God does not allow us to pick and choose when we will share our gifts and who will be the recipient. Growing up to the Head in His love means not using God's gifts in a discriminatory manner. Too many church members have gifts hidden under the pews. Some have the gift of encouragement but are not encouraging anybody. Some have the gift of help but are not helping anybody. Some have the gift of teaching and not teaching anywhere in the church. Many have the gift of administration but are not utilizing it. Some have the gift of leadership and are not leading. Some have the gift of evangelism but are not sharing the love of God and Gospel of Jesus with a lost and dying world.

Growing up to the Head in His love means sharing in love.

Growing up to the Head in His love means sharing in love. Some may have a gift or talent, to a greater or lesser degree. God pays attention to what we do with what we have. Remember that Jesus called upon Peter to feed His sheep, even though the degree of love He had for Christ was less than what He was calling for.

THE GREATEST GIFT

The greatest gift we have been given is love. It is easy for the Jesus in me to love the Jesus in you. God is love. Love is God. God's gift to the world is love. The Book of Matthew (22:36-40) records a conversation between Jesus and a lawyer: "Master, which is the greatest commandment in the law? Jesus

181

said unto him, Thou shalt love the Lord thy God with all thy heart, and with all thy soul, and with all thy mind. This is the first and great commandment. And the second is like unto it, Thou shalt love thy neighbour as thyself. On these two commandments hang all the law and the prophets." The Book of Luke records this conversation in a slightly different manner. After Jesus tells the greatest and second greatest commandments, he told the story of the Good Samaritan, whose actions were motivated by love. The other men in this passage who had passed the fallen man were considered to be very religious, yet their righteousness was not rooted in love. They could not translate their righteousness into action to help a fallen human being. Everything we are to do as disciples hinges on love. Every deed, every act must be grounded in love.

Everything we are to do as disciples hinges on love.

Paul closes 1 Corinthians 13 by reminding us that some gifts will cease, yet faith, hope and love will abide. Many people read 1 Corinthians 13 as part of their marital vows. But the context of the chapter really deals with spiritual gifts. Paul is saying that it doesn't matter what abilities we have, what talents we have, what gifts we have been given. If our love does not motivate us to use those gifts, they are worth nothing. A woman may have the voice of a songbird; yet if she does not love, her gift is worthless. A man may have the gift for serving others; but if he does not love, his gift is worth nothing.

In Paul's discourse on love, it is interesting that a lot of those gifts started out together, but love ended up being the champion. I like to make the analogy to Division I NCAA basketball. Each year we experience March Madness with the playoffs for college basketball. They start competition with sixty-four teams and, through a process of elimination, decrease downward through the Sweet Sixteen and the Elite Eight until there are only four teams remaining, the Final Four. Paul narrowed the most important gifts down to the final three. But it is interesting that in the first round, many gifts were eliminated. In the first round, speaking in tongues got eliminated. The gift of tongues became like sounding cymbals and tinkling brass because if you don't have love, speaking in tongues means nothing. In another round, the gift of prophecy got eliminated; and in yet another round, manner and benevolence were eliminated.

There are many gifts, but the final three—faith, hope and love—are lasting gifts. Even of the final three, the greatest is love. At one time, it bothered me that faith would be eliminated because without faith it is impossible to please God. I could not understand how faith could ever lose. But I came to the spiritual discernment that after I die, I will be looking at the great Justifier so I don't really need faith anymore. Also, I was troubled by the fact that hope was eliminated. Since I will be looking at the One who I hope to see, I won't need hope anymore. When I close my eyes and wake up again, I will awaken in the arms of love. Love is the greatest gift of all. Love is the only thing that can help us. Growing up to the

Love is the greatest gift of all. Love is the only thing that can help us.

Head in love means knowing that nothing surpasses God's love.

APPLICATION

How shall our love bring forth a harvest of growth in our churches? We have to show God's love before we can tell about God's love. When we attempt to tell oth-

We have to show God's love before we can tell about God's love.

ers the Good News, we must remember that our credibility as a Christian must first be earned. The late Mother Teresa, known worldwide for her life of love and sacrifice, said, "True acts of love go before God forever as worship to Him." Americans, particularly in the Bible Belt, have grown accustomed to being preached at. Far too few who are outside of the body know what it is like to be "loved at." To phrase love as "loving at," puts the word in verb form. Too often, we leave love as simply a feeling, not as an act. What would happen if, instead of preaching, judging, and condemning, we started simply loving those who do not know Christ. I don't mean a distant kind of love for humankind that says, "I love you because the Bible says I must, but don't ask me to help you." I'm talking about the kind of love which motivates us to take action.

In a book entitled *Conspiracy of Kindness* (Servant Publications, 1993), author Steve Sjogren expands on evangelism as an outpouring of love. What Sjogren addresses is not something he originated. Rather, he helps readers refocus on what evangelism is all about: it is sharing God's message of love and the Good News of salvation through Jesus Christ. Growing up in His love is knowing that evangelism means living the Good News as well as telling it. Certainly, church growth does occur through evangelism, or spreading the Good News.

> *When we have grown up in His love, we know that every believer has a responsibility to share the Good News.*

Sjogren explains that Christians have many myths concerning evangelism. He challenges readers to learn to do evangelism "Samaritan-style." But in order to do Samaritan-style witnessing, each person must understand that evangelism is not picking those who look like good candidates for the Kingdom. Evangelism is not throwing the responsibility on the preacher or the deacons. When we have grown up in His love, we know that every believer has a responsibility to share the Good News. Evangelism is more than simply giving out a tract which explains eternal life or eternal damnation. A pamphlet on eternal damnation doesn't mean anything to a starving man. What does mean something to him is something to eat. If you love him enough to feed him, you have opened his mind to hearing the message of love.

It is the experience of love which opens the human heart to the message of love. For instance, the message of the pro-life movement will be heard more strongly if equal concern and compassion is shown for the born as well as the unborn. Recently, a woman shared a personal experience which caused her great distress. Her unmarried, teenage daughter had recently given birth prematurely. The woman asked the head of the agency where she worked to excuse her from attending an annual conference in order to stay in town and be near her daughter and her premature grandchild. The head of this agency had achieved national attention for his pro-life stance. He refused her request even though her participation in the event would be minimal. She wondered how he could claim support for the unborn yet seem so unconcerned about the newly born. The woman said to me, "My daughter decided to have the baby and not an abortion. Shouldn't she be getting support for her decision? Does his concern only extend to unborn babies? What about after they are born?" This woman was frustrated because the loving words which she had been hearing were not supported by loving actions. Growing up to the Head in His love means being pro-life for both the born and the unborn. Growing up to the Head in His love means being supportive in both word and action.

> *Growing up to the Head in His love means being supportive in both word and action.*

A pastor I know told a story about a beautiful, well-dressed woman who walked down the aisle to join his church. When she gave her testimony, she revealed that she had recently been released from incarceration. For the years she was in jail, that church provided Christmas presents for her children without fail. Upon her release from prison, she wanted to align herself with the congregation who had demonstrated consistent love and concern for those whom she loved. That church's love won that woman to Christ.

> *If your church does not do ministry in love, your loving members will look elsewhere for a church home.*

A man I know has a son who is learning disabled. He has often said, unapologetically, that if he could not find a church that had a place for his son, he would not go to church either.

Church growth occurs when we love others and the people whom they love.

If your church does not do ministry in love, your loving members will look elsewhere for a church home. A church that is unable to experience love will not have loving members. A church without loving members will not greet visitors with kindness. A church without loving members will not go out seeking lost sheep. A church without loving members will not use their gifts as a means of showing God's love.

FOR STUDY AND REVIEW

Chapter Six
Growing Up to the Head in His Love

1. There are three Greek words for the English word "love." List them below:

   _____, _____, _____

2. How does growing up to the Head in His love affect our relationships with family, coworkers, friends, church members and strangers?

3. Below, write the definition of love as a "noun" and then as a "verb."
   (a) Love (noun) -

   (b) Love (verb) -

4. Real love for Jesus is evidenced by a _____ relationship.

5. Godly love, *agape*, often involves _____.

6. Read John 3:16. God exhibited His love through the act of
   _____.

7. Spiritual gifts are the supernatural ability, given to every believer by God, to build the church by building up one another. How have you used your spiritual gifts to build up yourself, your family, your church and your community?

8. Everything we are to do as disciples hinges on _____.

9. Growing up in His love is knowing that evangelism means _____ the Good News as well as _____ it.

Growing Up in His Word

1. Read John 21:15-19. What type of love was Peter talking about? What type of love was Jesus talking about? Can Jesus' request to Peter be carried out without the type of love Jesus was referring to? Explain your answer.

2. Re-read Ephesians 3:19. Explore what it means to be loved and to extend love which surpasses your human ability to understand.

Growing Up Together

A church growing up to the Head in His love is comprised of individuals growing up spiritually. Discuss how your church is viewed in your community and why. What can be done or what areas can be improved upon which will identify your church as being one that exhibits unconditional love?

Growing Up to the Head!

Read Romans 5:8. Re-read John 3:16. Understanding how God exhibited His love for you, how do you plan to share that love with others so that you may exhibit your process of growing up to the Head in love?

GROWING UP TO THE HEAD

In His Likeness

When we have been touched by the Savior, we are no longer the same. From the time we accept Him as Lord and Savior, we begin a process of trans-

> *And that ye put on the new man, which after God is created in righteousness and true holiness. Ephesians 4:24*

formation. We are to grow toward His likeness. Growing up in His likeness means paying less attention to the desires of the flesh and more attention to His will for us. Ephesians 4:17-24 addresses this process of renewal as we strive to become more like Him.

In verse 22, Paul says our old nature is corrupt. The word corrupt can be literally translated as "perishing." It is a verb translated into what is known in English as present participle. This verb form suggests a progressive decay. The old nature is continuously dying as the new grows stronger.

Paul says that, because we now know Him, we can no longer act or think like people who don't know Him. People who don't

Growing up in His likeness means knowing our human mind is not to be trusted.

know the Lord think that they are calling the shots. They think they can use their mental capacity to process anything that happens. Paul calls this vanity. Their understanding has been darkened (or clouded) because they are apart from God and are, therefore, ignorant. The pitiful part is that they don't even know they're in darkness because they are depending on their human minds to get them through life.

In Romans 1:18-32, Paul paints a picture of the pagan lifestyle, a portion of which reads, "Because that, when they knew God, they glorified him not as God, neither were thankful; but became vain in their imaginations, and their foolish heart was darkened. Professing themselves to be wise, they became fools, And changed the glory of the uncorruptible God into an image made like to corruptible man, and to birds, and fourfooted beasts, and creeping things (vs. 21-23)." Leaning on our own mind causes us to act like fools. Proverbs 3:5 tells us to "trust in the LORD with all thine heart; and lean not unto thine own understanding." Growing up in His likeness means knowing our human mind is not to be trusted. There have been many times in my life when I felt I had perfect recollection of an event. In my mind, I knew I had it right. Later on, I realized that I had it all wrong. The human mind cannot be trusted. Even when we try our best and are filled with good intentions, we cannot be trusted.

Several things happen when we attempt to trust the human mind. The first is that our understanding is darkened. We cannot see spiritual realities clearly. Second, when we try to get through this life on the strength of the human mind, we suffer alienation from God. The second consequence leads to the third, which is ignorance of God's way. When we don't know God's way, our hearts are hardened and we refuse to submit to the Almighty. Finally, when we are separated from God we cannot hear His voice calling to us, and that leads us to an unfeeling state. We then have gone too far. We can no longer hear His voice leading us through the paths of righteousness for His name sake.

Growing up in His likeness means trusting the divine Mind and forsaking human thinking.

For instance, a child may unknowingly step away from the hearing range of a parent's protective voice while they are in the mall. The child does not realize he is headed for all types of possible danger. He is using his thinking mind. In his mind, the mall seems like a nice, safe place with music, lights and people. He does not know that there are people who kidnap little boys and girls who are separated from their parents.

As believing adults, we need to stay within hearing range of our heavenly Father. We cannot possibly know all the ways He protects us. When we move away from Him, we must try to figure things out for ourselves with minds that cannot be trusted. The pagans Paul addressed in Ephesians were insensitive to God and didn't have sense enough to fear the consequences of their actions. Growing up in His likeness means trusting the divine Mind and forsaking human thinking.

Human thinking gets us into trouble. How many times have you looked at some of the choices you have made and said, "I thought it was the right thing to do." Human thinking told Peter that Jesus should not die on the cross (Matthew 16:22). Human thinking motivated James and John to ask Jesus to place them on His right and left sides (Mark 10:35-41). Jesus let them know they really did not want what they were asking for. Jesus' divine mind knew that He had to "drink from the cup." Equipped with only a human mind, James and John could never have arrived at that conclusion. Jesus also let them know that it was not His choice to make.

Although we never can, we should strive to grow into His steps.

Because He was also divine, Jesus knew that some things were beyond His humanness. But even Jesus was not exempt from human thinking. His humanness caused Him to ask, "O my Father, if it be possible, let this cup pass from me: nevertheless not as I will, but as thou wilt" (Matthew 26:39).

WALKING IN HIS STEPS

Have you ever seen a little girl try to walk in her mother's high heel shoes? Because they are too big for her, she wobbles as she tries to walk in them. She may trip a couple of times; nevertheless, she keeps trying to walk in those shoes, just like she has seen her mother do. There is something appealing to her about the way her mother walks in those shoes. She wants to grow up to those shoes ... she wants to grow up to be able to walk like her mother walks. That's what we should be doing as children of God. The shoes won't fit us, but we should still keep trying—getting bigger and better as we go. Eventually, our feet grow to fit those shoes better. We should never stop striving to grow into His steps.

In a book written by Charles M. Sheldon in 1896 entitled *In His Steps*, the author tells a fictitious yet true-to-life story. It depicts the life of almost any congregation. The book begins with a pastor of a local church preparing his sermon. The preacher was at home, struggling to get his quiet time to prepare his sermon. A man who appeared to be a tramp showed up about that time. He was not dressed the way the pastor and his congregants would dress; he was somewhat ragged. The pastor turned him away. The man then went down to another church, and the people there basically ignored him. On Sunday morning, the man showed up for worship. He gave an impromptu speech, very intelligent and right to the point, speaking of the hard times which had befallen him. Technology had displaced him, so his job skills were no longer marketable. He had looked for other kinds of work but could not find any. He said he came to the church because he had been taught that this was the place where people do what Jesus would have done. Then he collapsed in the sanctuary. Some worshippers took him to the pastor's study where they were able to revive him. Then they took him to the pastor's house to nurse him and restore him. While there, he passed away. In the pastor's heart, and in the congregation's heart, were those words that the man had relayed to them right before the communion table: "What would Jesus do? I thought I was in a place where people say that they are following in His steps. What would Jesus have done if I showed up in front of Him?"

The pastor was so convicted that he asked for anybody who would come for a commitment time to meet with him. This was a church that had some influential members, who were in high profile places. Much to his surprise, some people he did not

> *Growing up to His likeness means measuring our every decision against the question, "What would Jesus do?"*

expect to show up came. He asked them for a commitment: "For one year, in all your decisions, in all the things you do, would you first ask the question, 'What would Jesus have done?'" By the spirit of God that rests with you, ask yourself, "What would Jesus have done?" Then do it! Regardless of the consequences. Do it anyway. Some fifty persons committed to do this. Can you imagine having fifty people who would commit, for one year, to measure every decision they make against "what would Jesus do"? Growing up to His likeness means measuring our every decision against the question, "What would Jesus do?"

The first challenge came from a man who was the owner, publisher and editor-in-chief of a newspaper. There was a prize fight in town that was the biggest thing happening. It was headline news, but he told his reporters, "Don't report it." They thought he was crazy. The newspaper boys were shouting the headlines in the street. People were reading the headlines, looking for news about the fight, but there was nothing there. The paperboys were upset because they couldn't sell their papers. People went and bought other papers. People started saying, "You will go out of business running a newspaper like this." The publisher still paid the newspaper boys because, even though they didn't sell any papers, he thought that's what Jesus would have done.

All of us ought to be willing to take some risks. Jesus took a lot of risks and stood up against the "establishment" of His day. Growing up in His likeness means being willing to take

Growing up in His likeness means evaluating all our activity against what Jesus would do.

some risks. Just like the pastor and those fifty people in his church, we ought to look at things differently as we grow closer to His likeness. We should begin doing things like Jesus did. For the rest of our lives, we ought to be walking in His steps, growing up in His likeness. In everything we do, with each and every decision we make about each and every thing in life, we should base it on what Jesus would have done, and then suffer the consequences. Deal with the results. Our challenge is to grow up in His likeness by walking in His steps. Growing up in His likeness means evaluating all our activities against what Jesus would do.

Throughout the rest of Sheldon's book, people's lives were being upset all because those fifty people had decided they would do as Jesus would have done; they were causing some problems for other folks. Everybody wasn't happy that these people were making life choices according to what Jesus would have done. In other words, some people weren't happy because these people had decided to grow up in His likeness. That's important for each of us to remember in real life. Growing up in His likeness will not necessarily cause others to be pleased with us. Often, those closest to us—spouse, parents, children, relatives, co-workers and neighbors—will be the ones who object to what we have decided to do for Him. Satan knows our weak spot. That's why Satan chose Peter to tell Jesus that He should not die on the cross. Satan will use your mama, your daddy, your husband, your wife, your boss and any-body else he thinks will do the trick. Satan uses them, and they don't even know it. That's why Jesus said we have to be willing to forsake family and loved ones for Him. That's why Jesus told the man, "Follow me; and let the dead bury their dead" (Matthew 8:22). Growing up in His likeness means we

To do what Jesus would have done requires growing up to the Head in His likeness.

may have to forsake everyone to follow Him.

To do what Jesus would have done requires growing up to the Head in His likeness. You have to know Him to be like Him. Scientists study diseases all the time to determine what they will do. They need to know the likely pattern of a disease so they can reasonably predict its pattern in the human body. We need to know Jesus so that we can predict His pattern. We need to know what He would do before we can try to replicate His behavior. If a 40-year-old actor is going to play the part of a 90-year-old man, he will begin spending time around men

...we must study the habits of our Lord, through His Word in order to grow up in His likeness.

who are around that age. He needs to know how a 90-year-old man moves—how he thinks and what he believes. The actor has to do all this so that he can replicate the behavior of an old man. Likewise, we must study the habits of our Lord through His Word, in order to grow up in His likeness.

AN EPISTLE LESSON

First Peter 2:21 tells us, "To this were you called, because Christ suffered for you, leaving you an example that you should follow in his steps." To get a better understanding of that verse, a little background information might be helpful.

In the day that God led Peter to write this general Epistle, Christians were under much persecution. As a matter of fact, it was a crime just to be a Christian. They were living in a hostile world, and Nero had determined to punish all Christians. Oftentimes, Christians would be wrapped in animal fur, set on fire and then rolled down the streets of Rome like human fireballs. The general goal of the Epistle was to encourage Christians who were living under these hostile conditions.

The Epistle was also written for us today because we, too, live in a hostile world where right is in the minority and wrong is in the majority. Wickedness has not ceased from troubling, and the devil is having a heyday—a heyday in the newspapers, at the movies, in magazines, on television, at the video stores, in corporate America and even in the Christian church. He's got us believing that we're not one Church but many churches.

You can not have competition among churches and grow up in His likeness.

One day I picked up a magazine that had the name of our church in it. But it had churches rated in relationship to their choirs: the fifty greatest choirs in Atlanta. I believe that this is the

We need to crave the Word of God so that we can grow up and walk in His steps and in His likeness.

deceptive work of the devil. Jewish people have one temple, but we have many churches. That weakens us. I don't want to pastor the biggest and the greatest church, I want to follow in His likeness! You can not have competition among churches and grow up in His likeness. Growing up in His likeness means realizing that the church is one body and a body does not fight against itself; so there should be no competition among Christian churches for choirs, members or anything.

Peter was writing to church people in the Book of 1 Peter. He was saying, "Now that you are saved you ought to grow up in your salvation." We ought to grow up in His likeness. God gives us an illustration that we ought to be hungering for the Word, just like a new born baby hungers and craves for his mother's breast. A mother feeding her child is a beautiful event. I grew up on an agricultural campus and saw the animals give birth. The little pigs would scramble to see who could get to the mother for milk. The runt of the litter could never get there. We would have to take the runt and put him where he could get some more milk. Just as all the little pigs were scrambling for milk, we ought to be scrambling, now that we've tasted, and we know that the Lord is good. Now that He's saved us ... now that we've been born again...now that we've been washed in the blood of the lamb, we need to crave the Word of God. We need to be scrambling for Sunday School. We need to be hurrying to church on Sunday morning and on Wednesday night so that we can grow up in His likeness.

We need to crave the Word of God so that we can grow up and walk in His steps and in His likeness. Our problem is that we can't decide who we want to look like. You look at some children and they bear a greater resemblance to one parent than the other. You say something like, "She favors her mother" or "He favors his father." Who do you look like? Do you favor your heavenly Parent (God) or do you favor His adversary?

There is the beat of the world, and as Dr. Martin Luther King, Jr. said, "You need to march to the beat of a different drummer." I'm talking about Jesus Christ our Lord. Who is your drum major? The drum major is the one out front. He's leading the band. Satan is a drum major, but Jesus is the best Drum Major. Is He leading you? Are you marching to His beat? Does He show you the way to go, or are you going your own way? Are you watching His steps so that you can imitate them? Growing up in His likeness means marching to the beat of a different drummer.

LIFE IN CHRIST

In Ephesians 4:20, Paul provides a contrast of the life of a pagan with that of one who is in Christ. Basically, Paul is saying, "This way of life, living in darkness and so forth, does not fit into the life of one who is in Christ."

Growing up to His likeness means the power of Christ will control our selfish desires.

When we grow up in His likeness, the words of Christ will be in our mind and our heart—the love of Christ will be behind our every action and behavior. Growing up to His likeness means the power of Christ will control our selfish desires. The Word and

Growing up to His likeness means the power of Christ will control our selfish desires.

the way of Christ will be forever in our mind. The love of Christ will guide our every action. Everything we do will be motivated by our love for Christ.

There are basically three methods through which people attempt to have a life in Christ Jesus. Two of those three methods won't work; they are no good. Two of the three will send you to hell. The first one is what I call a "life of legalism." That's when you think you can be saved by keeping the law. Many people live a life of legalism while professing belief in Jesus. Still, they believe that they can be saved simply by doing perfectly everything that Jesus said for us to do. The problem with that is that we cannot live a sinless life. Our very nature is sinful. Second, even if we could, there is no salvation in the law. But many people think they are living in Christ when all they are really doing is living in legalism. It amounts to what I call "negative goodness." My terminology is an oxymoron, but it's true. The behavior may be good because the person does all the things the Bible says. However, it's negative because the doing depends on the person and not upon Christ. Negative goodness will keep a person in turmoil and will eventually lead that person to hell.

The second method people claim as life in Christ is what I call a "life of license." Many people live the Christian life by a method of license. They think that, because of grace, they've got a license to do anything they want. That cheapens grace. Grace does not give us a license to sin. We have been set free *from* sin, but we have not been set free *to* sin. In Galatians 5:13, Paul says,

Life in Christ is filled with love, but life apart from Him is filled with legalism and frustration.

"Ye have been called unto liberty, only use not liberty for an occasion to the flesh..." In other words, "Don't use your freedom to sin." Like a life of legalism, a life of license will cause pain now and will eventually lead the person who tries to live this way to hell.

But yet there is a third way of living. The life in Christ is a life of liberty. A life of liberty gives you the power over sin but does not free you to go out and sin. Because we love God, we are guided by the Holy Spirit to a life of liberty, and the words of Christ will be in our mind. When we do not have a life in Christ, we have no real, everlasting peace ... no joy, just turmoil. Eventually, a life apart from Him means everlasting hell. In other words, hell now and hell later. People have often said, "I'm living in hell." But they're living in hell for a reason. God's children have no business living in hell because that is the result of an individual trying to live a life apart from Christ. That kind of life is hell now and hell later. That's the only possible result for the individual. Life in Christ is filled with love, but life apart from Him is filled with legalism and frustration.

Trying to live the Christian life by any way other than in Him will lead us to what I call Christian cannibalism. Paul says in Galatians 5:15, "But if you bite and devour one another, take heed that ye be not consumed one of another." He's talking about Christian cannibals eating and devouring one another. It happens all the time in the church. Somebody tries to judge somebody else. Somebody tries to determine how many marriages another person has had. Somebody's trying to determine how many divorces someone else has had. Somebody's trying to determine how many babies someone else had out-of-wedlock.

Judging one another ultimately becomes gentle legalism (negative goodness), and it will certainly lead to Christian cannibalism. In a church of legal license, the preacher and the deacons

Growing up in His likeness means we have no desire to devour another's spirit.

may think that, because of grace, they have a license to date every sister in the choir. That will eventually lead to spiritual devouring; we will kill one another's spirit like animals. Growing up in His likeness means we have no desire to devour another's spirit. When we grow up in His likeness, we only desire the best for one another, as He desires only the best for us.

RIGHT THINKING

We must grow up to His likeness and into His mind. In other words, we have to think right: "But that ye be perfectly joined together in the same mind and in the same judgment" (1 Corinthians 1:10). You can't live right until you think right. How do you have the right kind of thinking?

There are three steps we must take to develop the right kind of thinking. The very first step is to be transformed by the renewing of your mind. Romans 12:2 says, "Be not conformed to the world but be ye transformed by the renewing of your mind." Paul's environment was inundated with Greek philosophy, which deals with the mind. The very essence of who we are

Growing up in His likeness means becoming as the mind of Christ.

comes out of our minds, so we must deal with the renewing of the mind. If we are going to control the old nature, it requires a renewing of what makes us tick—the very essence of who we are. That's how we live a life in Christ. We have to be transformed by the renewing of our mind so we can walk in the Spirit. Growing up in His likeness means becoming as the mind of Christ.

The second step is that we must treat the flesh ruthlessly. Paul says, "And they that are Christ's have crucified the flesh with the affections and lusts" (Galatians 5:24). That's the finished work of Christ. When Christ died on the cross, He crucified the flesh. We're to follow suit, growing up in His likeness. Treat the flesh ruthlessly. What I'm saying is, "Don't tempt the flesh—don't mess with the flesh in the flesh's territory." In other words, stay out of your flesh's red light district. It may be Las Vegas, if you can't control your gambling. The red light district may be Neiman Marcus and Macy's, if you can't control your spending and consumption. The red light district may be the local buffet restaurant, if you can't control your eating. Your red light district may be the night club or the jazz club. Maybe it's HBO or late night pay-per-view television. Don't give the flesh any opportunities to sin. Don't give the flesh home court advantage. Avoid sinful opportunities and territory when it comes to working with the flesh. This is spiritual warfare! Don't give the flesh the upper hand.

Third, if we are to develop the right kind of thinking, we must starve the flesh and feed the Spirit. When you have a garden, you don't need to feed the weeds to make them grow. What makes the weeds grow? Nothing, they just grow. If you want your flowers or vegetables to grow, you'd better try to starve the weeds. Likewise, starve the flesh and feed the Spirit. Don't watch violence if you have a bad temper. Don't read *Playboy* and *Playgirl* or toy with pornography. Don't watch soap operas with Sally going with Johnny and Johnny going with Barbara and Barbara going with Peggy

Use every tool necessary to put yourself in the posture of right thinking.

and Freddie going with Teddie. Cut up your credit cards if you can't handle them. Set your affections on Christ. Set your love on Christ. Use every tool necessary to put yourself in the posture of right thinking. That's what got the pagans in trouble in Ephesians. They thought they could handle everything on their own. Christ was nowhere near them.

When bad habits are defeating you, it's time to get a whole new set of habits. It's time to replace the old for the new. Become a new person. Stay in His mind and you will abide in Him. If you abide in Him, you will grow up in His likeness. Have quiet time with God every day. Read your Bible and pray every day. Stay near the fellowship of God's people. Go to Sunday School. Don't forsake the assembling of the body. Go to church every Sunday. Have private praise time with God. Get somewhere in your closet and just praise God. Let your Spirit shout within you. Can your Spirit shout when you are all alone? When you're home alone, feed the Spirit by listening to some good praise music. Memorize and internalize a verse of Scripture every day. Feed the Spirit and starve the flesh!

A NEW CREATURE

Some of us have seen a discarded snakeskin lying on the ground. It was discarded and left behind because it was not needed. The snake has formed a new skin which caused it to outgrow the old one. We can compare our old and new nature in much the same way. The old person, the person before Christ, should be shedding away. Our new self, formed in Christ Jesus, should cause us to outgrow the old self. The old self should be too small to contain the new self that we have become in Christ.

Ephesians 4:22-23 talks about getting rid of the old man and being renewed. Because they knew Christ, the Ephesians had learned new, life-altering truths. Paul is saying that, because of their knowledge in Christ, they could not possibly live as they did before they knew Him. When each of us encounters Christ, we are to allow the Holy Spirit to renew our ways of thinking, changing them from impure to holy. Growing up to the Head in His Likeness is about outgrowing the old self and making room for the new self.

If we grow up in His likeness, we can rise with Him.

If we grow up in His likeness, we can rise with Him. We want to follow in His spiritual steps. In order to do so, we must take up our crosses daily and follow Him. The old nature doesn't want to take up that cross, but the new man Christ created does. The old nature wants pleasure, not a cross. Sometimes the old nature battles with the new man. Sometimes the old man has to "duke it out" with the new man Christ made. Still, every believer will retain his or her old nature of the flesh; we will not get rid of it in this lifetime. Every disciple, no matter how long they've been walking with the Lord, still has the old nature of the flesh.

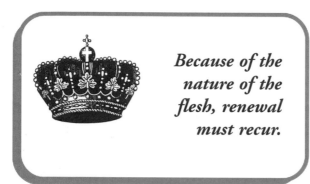

Because of the nature of the flesh, renewal must recur.

In John 3:6 Jesus said to Nicodemus, "That which is born of the flesh is flesh, that which is born of the Spirit is Spirit." The idea that we will get rid of the old nature is a crucial mistake in Christianity. You can control the old nature, but you don't get rid of the old nature. First John 1:8 says, "If we say that we have no sin, we deceive ourselves, and the truth is not in us." In other words, God is saying that anyone who thinks he or she is so holy and without sin is a liar. From the pulpit and everywhere else, anyone who says, "I have no sin," is engaging in self-deception, and the truth is not in that person.

In Ephesians 4:22, Paul does not say the old nature will disappear. Instead, he admonishes us to put it aside, like an old suit that is no longer of use to us. Paul is not addressing the heathen here. One who is outside of Christ doesn't even know what Paul is talking about. Here, Paul is making his appeal to those who have known renewal of the Spirit, which began at conversion. This renewal is a continuous process. Paul calls for the continuous process of renewal. It is not a "one shot deal." Because of the nature of the flesh, renewal must recur. Paul has said that the flesh wars against the Spirit.

Many of us associate the word "flesh" primarily with lust or sexual sins. The meaning of "flesh" is so much deeper. Flesh has to do with whatever desirous appetites you might have that would cause you not to grow up in His likeness. Even the word "lust" has to do with that which would take the place of spiritual things.

> *Flesh has to do with whatever desirous appetites you might have that would cause you not to grow up in His likeness.*

Lust can very easily refer to things that we don't think of as immoral, such as music, sports, recreation, religion. None of those are evil in themselves, but when they take the place of spiritual things, they become the work of the flesh. Watching television can become the work of the flesh. Watching soap operas can be just as much the work of the flesh as looking at pornography. Idolatry—worshiping something other than God—is sin. Worshiping the Law is sin. There are social sins: rivalry, jealousy, wrath, hot-temperedness, strife, and sedition, which is creating factions and division. Forming cliques in the church is sin. Having factions in the choir is sin. You don't have to be guilty of adultery or fornication in order to sin. There are numerous things which constitute the old nature. Paul is telling us to put these things aside.

You may be thinking, "I've already put those things away. Now what do I do?" The renewal process does not end with simply putting the old nature away. When the old nature is cast

Growing up to the Head in His likeness means being filled with the newness of life.

aside, we must fill it with the new nature that has been imparted to us by faith in Christ Jesus. Human nature does not deal with vacuums. If we lose something, we find something to replace it. People who lose the ability to see gain a greater sense of hearing or smell. People who lose their legs get stronger in their arms. A parent who has lost a child may give herself or himself to volunteering to help other children. When there is a vacuum in our lives, we will find a way to fill it. Even a vacuum that was once filled with negative things must be refilled. And, guess what? If we don't soon fill the vacuum with something positive, something negative will return to haunt us. We are going to fill ourselves and our time with something. Paul is telling us to be careful to fill it with the new nature in Christ. Growing up to the Head in His likeness means being filled with the newness of life.

In Luke 11:24-26, Jesus tells the story of a man who gets rid of an evil spirit and replaces it with nothing: "When the unclean spirit is gone out of a man, he walketh through dry places, seeking rest; and finding none, he saith, I will return unto my house whence I came out. And when he cometh, he findeth it swept and garnished. Then goeth he, and taketh to him seven other spirits more wicked than himself; and they enter in, and dwell there: and the last state of that man is worse than the first." If we are not careful to replace the old nature with the new, we may find ourselves in worse shape than we were before.

Maybe you stopped hanging out with your old gang "on the corner" since you found Jesus. What are you going to do to fill up that time? If you don't find something to do, you may end up doing something worse than hanging on the corner. You may end up living on the corner! Are you going to fill that time with Bible study? With volunteer work? With Christian service? What are you going to do to replace the old nature? What will you take on as a new man in Christ? As a new woman in Christ? What cross will you pick up and carry?

The nature of the cross you bear for Christ is that it is something you sign up for, like the old volunteer armed services. Don't misunderstand what your cross is. I'm not talking about the fact that you have a sickness that won't go away. That's not your

The nature of the cross you bear for Christ is that it is something you sign up for...

cross because you didn't ask for that. I'm not talking about an elderly mother that lives with you. I'm not talking about your wayward, prodigal child who just won't act right. I'm not talking about your spouse who's strung out on drugs. That is a burden, but it is not your cross because you did not ask for that. But I'm talking about the voluntary cross you pick. You pick it up by your will today—you reach for it and pick it up. Pick up the cross of Jesus. Pick up the life of Jesus. Volunteer to pick up the life that He died for on the cross. You have to volunteer for that cross. You have to volunteer to become the new person in Christ. Growing up to the Head in His likeness means deliberately, intentionally volunteering to pick the life that Jesus died for on the cross.

As the old nature is perishing, the new nature is evolving and being renewed continuously. It's like the old saying, "I'm not what I ought to be, but thank God I'm not what I used to be." As I indicated at the beginning of the chapter, the verb expressing the concept of perishing suggests a process. Likewise, the concept of renewal, in the Greek, suggests a process. In fact, every chapter of the Book of Ephesians has used the present participle verb form, "growing" because spiritual growth is a process. We will never "have grown," as it signals a sense of completeness. We will always be growing up to every aspect of Him, including His likeness. We should strive to grow more in His likeness at every point in our lives. Every event, every problem in our lives should be viewed as an opportunity for more "growing up to..." Growing up to the Head in His likeness means realizing that you will never be grown until the day of redemption.

Growing up to the Head in His likeness means we must be willing to change.

Some of us get frustrated with ourselves because we have not arrived at spiritual perfection. Anyone experiencing this can take heart in the fact that spiritual perfection does not occur in this life. Rather, we are always striving for it. It is a goal for which we reach. It is always higher than we can jump. It is always further than we can reach. We are growing up in His likeness, His image. This means we will never be Him or take the place of Him but will grow to be more like Him.

Growing up to the Head in His likeness means we must be willing to change. God does not automatically change us. Although God Almighty is omnipotent and omnipresent, He will not violate our will. We must willingly be a part of the renewal process. But we cannot do it alone. We cannot become what God wants apart from Him working in our lives to make us new. What

> *Growing up in His likeness means being an imitator of God, a "knock-off" of the Original.*

Christ does, however, is take the initiative to cause us to want to be like Him. When we respond and submit our desires to Him, He gives us new desires. The desires He gives to us are much greater than anything we could have imagined for ourselves.

IMITATORS OF CHRIST

Nearly every time a popular "designer" item comes on the market, some manufacturer comes along and makes an imitation of the same item. A few years ago, ladies were spending hundreds of dollars on Louis Vuitton, Fendi and Gucci handbags. But the ladies who could not afford those $250.00 purses went on the street corners and bought an imitation of those designer purses for about $50.00. Some of the imitations, or "knock-offs" as they are called, were very well made. Others could be spotted from a distance as impostors.

We Christians are like the imitation designer handbags. Ephesians 5:1 says, "Be imitators of God, therefore, as dearly loved children." We can never be God, but we can be imitators of God. Just like some of those knock-off handbags were pretty good imitations, we should strive to be the same way. We should live and conduct ourselves in a way that causes others to see the love of God in us because we have modeled ourselves after Him. Growing up in His likeness means being an imitator of God, a

If we imitate Him, if we are growing up in His likeness, we will do what He does.

"knock-off" of the Original.

As I've already indicated, there can be well-made knock-offs and there can be poorly made knock-offs. Christians should try to be quality imitations. Our service should allow people to see God all over us. Our love should allow others to see God all through us. Our giving should let others see God all around us. We should be a knock-off, a well-made imitation of Him. We should be a proud imitator of the Real Thing. In the movie "The Color Purple," the character played by Oprah Winfrey, Sophia, was recalling a day when Miss Celie, played by Whoopie Goldberg, came to her aid. Sophia explained, "When I see'd you ... I know'd the'y is a God."

Miss Celie had shown God's love to Sophia at a time when she could not see it on her own. Miss Celie was Sophia's glimpse of God that day. As Christians, people should see us and know there is a God because we have imitated Him so well. We can never be Him, but we can continue to grow up to Him in His likeness. God uses us to reveal Himself. We are not showing His likeness if we are engaged in sin. We have not shown His love by mistreating others.

If we imitate Him, if we are growing up in His likeness, we will do what He does. What does our Lord do? He loves people, He does not cast them aside because it's not convenient. Our Lord does not ridicule people to make them feel unworthy to enter the house of worship. Our Lord does not lie, cheat, and steal in an effort to get what He desires. He knows and trusts that His heavenly Father will grant all of these things. Our Lord seeks first the kingdom of God and His righteousness (Matthew 6:33). That means we first do what

Growing up in His likeness means taking no shortcuts to God's blessings by doing what is wrong.

God wants. It means we don't put aside doing God's business to attain a house, a job, a spouse or a political office. It means there are limits on what we will do in order to get the things we want. God will take care of providing the desires of our heart. Growing up in His likeness means taking no shortcuts to God's blessings by doing what is wrong. That's what people do when they want to be like Him. When we grow up in His likeness, we know that doing wrong to attain what is right is not necessary.

APPLICATION

How does growing up in His likeness apply to Kingdom-building and church growth? First, the congregation must remember the radical nature of the One they follow. If everyone

A church that is growing up in His likeness will remember His radical nature...

kept His nature close to heart, all will lay aside personal, or self-centered, interests and behave like there is something more important at stake than any single person in the congregation.

A church that is growing up in His likeness will remember His radical nature and will seek to replicate it in all of their ministries.

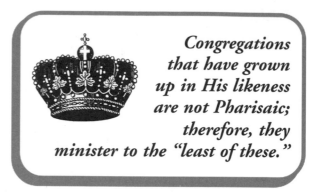

Congregations that have grown up in His likeness are not Pharisaic; therefore, they minister to the "least of these."

They will do radical things, like go among the people in the community or city and see what is lacking. They will listen and attempt to help and heal those who are hurting. A radical church will take the risk of stepping on tradition in order to help someone. In Luke 13, Jesus was criticized for healing the bent over woman on the Sabbath. That was a radical thing to do. The legalists had made the Sabbath most important. Jesus made the people in need most important.

Congregations that have grown up in His likeness are not Pharisaic; therefore, they minister to the "least of these." Jesus called His likeness the "least of these." In Matthew 25:40, our Lord says, "…Inasmuch as ye have done it unto one of the least of these my brethren, ye have done it unto me." Therefore, growing up in His likeness means ministering to the "least of these." Much of the trouble that Jesus had with the Pharisees stemmed from the fact that the Savior did not play their game of hierarchy. Jesus was not impressed by titles. No one person was any more important than another. If anything, He gave more attention to those who were lowest on the socio-economic ladder. Jesus was concerned with the needs of the least and the lowest. He regularly broke with the Law in order to show His love. Jesus put people above the law, even the "nobodys" of His time.

There are still churches around the globe that are more concerned about tradition than compassion. There are some churches that shun people who do not fit in a certain educational or economic class. They don't want certain kinds of people coming to their church. Several years ago,

> *Growing up in His likeness means embracing those who are on the lowest rung of the ladder of human success.*

when Andrew Young was mayor of Atlanta, he lived as a homeless man for a couple of days. One Sunday morning, he went to the parking lot of the church where he is a member. He was surprised at the people who turned away from him as they proceeded toward the sanctuary. The people who eagerly embraced him as mayor of Atlanta did not even want to make eye contact with him as one of the underclass. As much as this surprised Mayor Young, his church members probably did not react much differently than most church members across America. Growing up in His likeness means embracing those who are on the lowest rung of the ladder of human success.

A radical church may open its doors at odd hours in order to meet some needs. A radical church may step on or over tradition in order to meet some needs. I have often felt as though I was blessed by my background when I came to pastor Greenforest. I had never pastored a church before! Consequently, there were many things our church did because I didn't know they weren't supposed to be done. And, in spite of my ignorance about these long-held church traditions, our church grew by leaps and bounds. Growing up in His likeness means being willing to risk being criticized. Maybe your church wants to open a homeless shelter or a shelter for battered women and children but your community doesn't want "that sort of thing" there. The Pharisees and Sadducees didn't want what Jesus called "ministry" in their community either. But Luke 13 tells us that although He made the religious leaders angry, the people rejoiced in what Jesus had to say. Jesus said in John 10:10, "I am come that they might have life, and that they might have it more abundantly."

> *The Church cheapens Him by being tight-lipped about abundant living and loose-lipped on judgement.*

Is your church committed to helping people have abundant life? Very often, we're big on telling people who is going to hell. We're very big on picking out the ones who "don't know Jesus." We're masters at criticizing what someone did wrong. But how often do we preach, teach and live abundant life? Growing up in His likeness means abundant life. The Church cheapens Him by being tight-lipped about abundant living and loose-lipped on judgement. The church that gives of itself in imparting to others the abundant life, which comes through salvation in Christ Jesus, will be a growing church. People these days are living in a stingy world ... stingy with love ... stingy with helping ... stingy with forgiveness ... stingy with kind words ... stingy with giving. But, if someone goes out into that stingy world telling people about abundance, people are going to follow him or her. Jesus did it. Jesus had people following Him all the time because they knew good things were happening when He was around. Nobody was getting hurt when He was around. People got helped and healed when He

> *If we are growing up in His likeness, we must adopt an attitude of abundance.*

was around. Our Lord doesn't know how to give a little bit. There's no such thing as an "abundant little." That's another oxymoron. It doesn't make sense. If we are growing up in His likeness, we must adopt an attitude of abundance.

Too often, we in the church are like the world. The world is stingy, but the church is cheap. A stingy person is often that way because he or she doesn't have much. A stingy person is trying to hold on to the little that he or she already has. A cheap person is different. A cheap person has it but doesn't want to give it up. The Church is cheap. We have the abundance, but we don't want to give it away. We want to keep it for ourselves. You can't really blame the world for being stingy. They don't have any more to give. But the Church's crime is being cheap, being miserly, hoarding the Good News of abundant living. It's a message people are literally dying to hear. If we show them and tell them, they will flock to receive. People don't like living in a world of lack. (Maybe that's why some people are so angry at the church and won't go.) They know the church has the abundance but is hiding it, so no one on the outside can get to it. People are waiting to hear the Good News, and believers need to get out and tell it. Growing up in His likeness means telling the Good News—not just the bad news of hell, but the Good News of salvation. Salvation is good news, and God wants it for all His children. Our Lord has enough abundance for all of His children. It's like a magic vessel. The more we spread that abundance, the more abundance comes back to us to give away again. If we keep giving, we will keep growing.

> *Congregations that grow up to Him in His likeness follow His agenda.*

Congregations that grow up to Him in His likeness follow His agenda. Jesus' agenda was to seek and to save. Churches and church members should evaluate their activities, ministries and projects and determine whether or not they are following Jesus' agenda. Consideration should be given to eliminating all church projects, ministries, events and activities that do not contain components of Jesus' agenda. If a congregation has grown up to the Head in His likeness, it will apply the doctrine of the priesthood of believers to the governance of the church. When Jesus died on the cross, the curtain

> *...we no longer have the privilege of voting our own minds on issues related to the life of the church.*

was torn in the temple, giving all believers access to the Father in and through the Son. Therefore, we are all priests. We can go to the Father individually. "But ye are a chosen generation, a royal priesthood, an holy nation, a peculiar people; that ye should show forth the praises of him who hath called you out of darkness into his marvellous light" (1 Peter 2:9).

However, because we are priests, we no longer have the privilege of voting our own minds on issues related to the life of the church. We should only vote as God wills, leaning not on our own understanding, but discerning the will of God. Voting only the mind of Christ in church business will foster a mess-free church environment. A mess-free church environment will allow people to experience the riches of the fullness of the presence of Jesus in the church, and the church will grow.

At Greenforest, in an attempt to implement the above, we eliminated all church business meetings and conferences. In order that we might continue to carry out the business of the church, they were replaced by what we call "Holy Spirit discernment sessions." Is this only a matter of semantics? We think not. It is an attempt to apply the priesthood of the believer doctrine to our total church life. We encourage church members to discern the way Jesus would vote, and then to vote His mind. The body of Christ should have no mind other than its Head.

FOR STUDY AND REVIEW

Chapter Seven
Growing Up to the Head in His Likeness

1. Growing up in His likeness means paying less attention to the desires of the flesh and more attention to God's will for us. Describe what you believe to be God's will for you.

2. Your new nature should be getting _____ as your old nature is continually_____.

3. Growing up in His likeness means knowing our human mind is not to be trusted. List the four things that happen when we attempt to trust the human mind.

    (a)

    (b)

    (c)

    (d)

4. Growing up in His likeness means we must be willing to take some _____.

5. One condition for being like God is that you must first know God. What are some things you can do to "get to know" God?

6. There must be no _____ in the church because we are one body.

7. List the three methods people claim as "life in Christ."

    (a)

    (b)

    (c)

8. What is "Christian cannibalism"?

Growing Up in His Word

1. Growing up in His likeness requires right thinking. Write Romans 12:2 in the space below. What is God's primary method for renewing our minds?

2. Read Philippians 2:5-11 and Galatians 5:24. What is the relationship between the mind and the actions of the body? If God views us as a new creature in Christ at the point of salvation, why do we not always resemble that new creature?

Growing Up Together

Recognizing that we will never be God, we can continue to grow up in His likeness. Discuss some works of the flesh within a congregation which would not reflect the likeness of Christ to the world. What is the origin of these sinful conditions? How can the Church develop or sharpen the image it should have?

Growing Up to the Head!

In your quiet time, stand before a full length mirror. Ask yourself, "Do people tell me I look like my heavenly Father?" Ask God to reveal to you the characteristics you have like Him and what characteristics you still have of your old father, the devil.

GROWING UP TO THE HEAD

In His Spirit

There has been much debate within the Christian community about what our focus should be. Some say we should focus on "the word." You hear a lot of people talking about "the word." They talk about *being* in the word. The word

And be not drunk with wine, wherein is excess; but be filled with the Spirit.

Ephesians 5:18

"being" is a verb that implies action. It implies movement. As we stated in Essential #2 concerning grace, God defined Himself as a verb. He said, "I Am." Our elementary English teachers taught us that "am" is simply a form of the verb "to be." Therefore, if we are *being* in the word, that implies that our spirit is attracted to the word.

Among some of our fellow believers, there seems to be a desire to attach ourselves to the concreteness of God's word. God's word is a guiding light for our existence, but the danger lies in a desire to have the entire Christian experience begin and end in the Bible. With such people, the Bible is deified. The Bible is

Growing up to the Head in His Spirit is more than simply having spiritual experiences.

worshiped and not the One who created it. It is not surprising that, in these uncertain times, people are looking for a definitive word, something in black and white, which removes any room for doubt or questioning.

At the other end of the spectrum are those believers who define themselves as "spiritual." They tend to downplay the role of God's holy word, instead choosing to string together experiences. They want to connect or commune with the Spirit. They look for places and events that will be "Spirit-filled." They are big on the "high" of dwelling in the Spirit and the spiritual experience, but they devote little or no time to God's word or to reality.

The transfiguration was an awesome experience for the disciples who accompanied Jesus. The experience was so great that Peter wanted to built three tabernacles so that Jesus, Elijah and Moses could be there all the time. That is the nature of a spiritual experience. It is so wonderful, we don't want to "come back down" from it. Growing up to the Head in His Spirit is more than simply having spiritual experiences. We must grow up to His Spirit as we continue to strive for wholeness. When we have the Spirit without the word, we blow up; when we have the word without the Spirit, we dry up. But when we have the Sprit and the word, we grow up. The Spirit and the word are necessary for our growth and development. We cannot be sustained by trying to choose one over the other.

Growing up to the Head in His Spirit is an awesome task. Think of it as being filled with the Holy Spirit. Ephesians 5:17-

18 says, "Wherefore be ye not unwise, but understanding what the will of the Lord is. And be not drunk with wine, wherein in excess; but be filled with the Spirit." It is the will of God that we be filled with His Spirit.

What does it mean to be filled with His Spirit?

GOD'S WILL FOR EVERY CHRISTIAN

People ask me all the time, "What is God's will for my life?" I tell them, "I know what God's will is for your life and for my life, too." Then they say, "How do you know?" I simply respond, "Well, He told me in my spirit and He showed me in His word." Now, if you don't trust my spirit, I'm sure you trust the word of God. His word says be not unwise; some say be not foolish. This is God's will for our lives: Be not excessively drunk with wine, and be filled with the Holy Spirit. I don't know anything about your relationship with God. But of this I am sure ... I am 100 percent, positively, absolutely sure that God's will for your life and for my life is that we be filled with the Holy Spirit. This may be one of the most important things you will ever read in your Christian life. The most important thing you can know is God's will for your life on this earth.

God told us if we live in the Spirit, we ought to walk in the Spirit. If we are saved, we ought to live like it. God's will for our lives is to be filled. To illustrate my point, let me tell you a little about myself. I did not get saved until I was twenty-one years old. I went all the way through college unsaved. I sometimes made mockery of the Christian boys who were my classmates. When I tried to pledge a fraternity, they asked me if I believed in God, and I told them no. I told them I was an atheist. I didn't know what the word really meant then, but I had heard about atheists. So the fraternity brothers told me, "You've got to believe in God before you can be in our fraternity." I still said, "I don't believe." Then they said, "Well, tell a lie." That was all I wanted. I had them then. "You're the Christian," I said, "and you're telling me to lie." I took that and made fun.

When I did get saved, I was in my room preparing to do a lesson on the Virgin Mary. God spoke to my heart, and I believed in Jesus. It warmed me, and I was excited about it. I know the moment and the hour of my salvation. But there was nobody there to disciple me. There was no one there to even affirm with me that I was saved. That is possibly why I'm so bent out of shape on discipleship in my pastorate. I'm bent out of shape behind Sunday school, too. I'm burdened for it. I need to share something even more personal. When I began pastoring Greenforest Community Baptist Church seventeen years ago, I was not filled with the Holy Spirit. But God was patient and merciful, allowing me to grow up in His Spirit as I led that group of believers.

So that you can understand why I make that statement, let me give you an illustration to help you understand something about my background. Once, as a child, I was at church and a woman started shouting. She almost hit me in the head with her umbrella. I ducked under the pew. I asked my elders, "What's wrong?" or "What's going on?" They told me. "She is full of the Spirit." In my boy's mind, and in my intellect, if that was full of the Spirit, I didn't want any of that. So I spent the greater portion of my life, and some of my Christian life, doing what I call "stiff-arming" the Holy Spirit. That's a football term and almost a lost art. But when you stiff-arm, you have the ball in one hand, and you take the other hand and push your opponent away. The man atop the Heisman Trophy is posed in a position of someone who is stiff-arming. Many of us today are stiff-arming the Holy Spirit. We don't want Him to catch up with us.

Many of us today are stiff-arming the Holy Spirit.

Someone asked me a question once. It was the first question put before me that made me get desperate enough to ask God to fill me with the Holy Spirit. Maybe it will help you, too. It's been a recurrent question in my life. The question is, "What are you doing in your Christian life, that you could not do without the filling and the power of the Holy Spirit?" What are you accomplishing? What are you achieving in your life that you could

What are you doing in your Christian life, that you could not do without the filling and the power of the Holy Spirit?

not do without the filling and the power of the Holy Spirit? The question disturbed me; it bothered me; it even angered me. After all, I had methods, I had procedures, I have intellect. What did I need this supernatural dynamic for? After careful examination of the question, I came to the conclusion and conviction that I was doing very little or nothing that I could not do without the power of the Holy Spirit. And that which I was doing most often was being done without the filling of the Holy Spirit. What are you doing in your Christian life? What are you overcoming? What are you achieving that you know for sure you could not achieve without the filling of the Holy Spirit? You ought to know the difference.

When our church goes out to do evangelistic visitation, we knock on doors, and don't know who's going to be on the other side of that door. You've got to be filled with the Holy Spirit to do that in the 1990's. In order to keep from doing old-fashioned witnessing, some of us will rationalize it away. We'll say we can't do that these days because people are shooting each other and killing each other. All that's true. We excuse ourselves from the necessity for evangelistic witnessing by saying, "We'd better not go to anyone's house if we don't know who they are." Yes, you can go to someone's house unannounced. The only

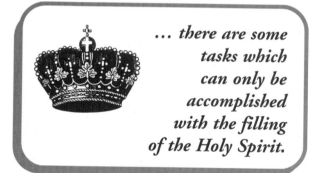

... there are some tasks which can only be accomplished with the filling of the Holy Spirit.

way you can do that, however, is with the power of the Holy Spirit. There are many other things that we can do when we are empowered by the Holy Spirit; going to a stranger's home to talk about Jesus is just one illustration. What bothers me is that Jehovah's Witnesses do it, and they don't even believe in the Holy Spirit! Yet we who claim to believe in the power of the Spirit can't muster up enough Holy Spirit to witness door-to-door. What are you doing? What are you doing in your Christian life that you could not do without the power of the Holy Spirit? Growing up in His Spirit means knowing that there are some tasks which can only be accomplished with the filling of the Holy Spirit.

Many of you with a Baptist background may be judging my theology right about now. If you are, let me unfold it a little for you. This is what I call sledge hammer theology. That's what you receive after God has told you something many times. Then, about the umpteenth time, He takes a sledge hammer and hits you in the head with it. Some of us fight yielding to the power and direction of the Holy Spirit. Some of us are hard-headed and want to do it our way and with our own power.

... you can't be filled with something or somebody you don't trust or you're scared of.

When God's gives us the sledge hammer, that's when we say, "Well, God, I never really thought about it like that before. I never saw it in that light before." Some of us don't pick up on things quite so quickly, and we need sledge hammer theology. God has shown it; we heard it. Yet, it takes the sledge hammer to get it within our theological thought. Many of us need sledge hammer theology because we've been in corporate America too long. Some of us need it because we've been listening to too much NLP, or neuro-linguistic programming. That's where your mind helps you visualize what you want to accomplish in life. Some of us have been trying to visualize what only the Holy Spirit can do. Our mind is stuck in NLP and needs a sledge hammer to knock us into the reality of the Holy Spirit. It is the Holy Spirit who guides and directs us, and not we ourselves.

FOUR REALITIES OF BEING SPIRIT-FILLED

I want to propose four realities for anyone trying to grow to be Spirit-filled. First, you can't be filled with something or somebody

Many of us are afraid of being Spirit-filled because we're afraid of losing control.

you don't trust or are afraid of. When we are afraid of something or someone, we spend our time trying to avoid it and protect ourselves from it. Many of us are afraid of being Spirit-filled because we're afraid of losing control. We are afraid of what may happen in our life if we let the Spirit take control. I've already confessed that I spent a good deal of my life grieving the Holy Spirit. I did not trust the Holy Spirit. We, in our twentieth century mindsets, have been programmed not to trust the leading of the Holy Spirit. We Baptists have been programmed against the Pentecostal church. We say to Pentecostals, "I'll take the Father, and I'll take the Son, but you take the Holy Ghost." Most of us "traditional" evangelicals have been programmed against Pentecostals. However, we need the Pentecostal church. We are all sisters and brothers in Christ. It is my belief that every church is a Pentecostal church. I also believe that every church is a missionary church. If we believe in Matthew 28:19, then every church is a missionary church. Likewise, if we believe in what happened in Acts 2, then every church is a Pentecostal church. We cannot "go ye therefore" and fulfill the command in Matthew 28:19 without the power of the Holy Spirit, promised to us in Acts 1:8.

Many of us don't want to wait on the leading of the Holy Spirit; we want an answer now. That kind of thinking has led to the proliferation of telephone psychics. It amazes me that people will call "psychic" hotlines to get a "reading," and they're not afraid. Every one of those psychic networks issues a disclaimer in small print at the bottom of the television screen indicating that they are "for entertainment purposes only." Yet, people are shouting prais-

... some of our churches are filled with people who trust the psychic reader more than the Holy Spirit.

es concerning the ability of these psychic readers to accurately foretell important events about their lives. Perhaps these hotlines are correct. Perhaps many of us simply want to be entertained. Many of us will trust important decisions in our lives to a reader whose primary job is "entertainment," but we will not trust the omnipotent One.

It's sad to think that some of our churches are filled with people who trust psychic readers more than the Holy Spirit. I know that it is possible because it is possible to build a church numerically without the Holy Spirit. Like the psychic hotlines, many churches should run a disclaimer in their Sunday bulletin, indicating that their function is "for entertainment purposes only." There are large churches across this country that are filled to the brim on Sunday morning, yet neither the churches nor their members are filled with the Holy Spirit.

The second reality is that some growth is certainly possible without the filling of the Holy Spirit. You can grow a church large in numbers without the Holy Spirit. You can grow a Sunday School class with many members without the Holy Spirit. You can grow a numerically large Bible study without the Holy Spirit. You can grow a numerically large prayer meeting without the power of the Holy Spirit. You can grow a huge choir without the filling of the Holy Spirit. With meth-

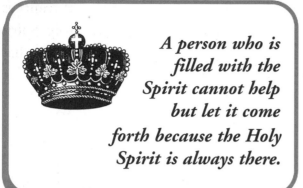

A person who is filled with the Spirit cannot help but let it come forth because the Holy Spirit is always there.

ods, procedures, job descriptions, well-defined roles and organization you can grow a church ministry and not be filled with the Holy Spirit. Growth in numbers is no indication of being Spirit filled. The church, Sunday School class, choir or other church organization that is numerically large but without the Holy Spirit is like a large package that has nothing inside. Often, such packages decorate the shopping malls during the Christmas holidays. The packages are beautifully and ornately decorated, yet they are empty. They have been all dressed up simply for effect.

Some of our churches are decorated purely for effect. Even some church members who claim to be filled with the Spirit are no more than ornate, empty packages. They may raise their hands and shout. They may say, "Amen." They may even do a holy dance every now and then. But they are only there for entertainment purposes. The Holy Spirit does not dwell in them. We should not be fooled by large building programs and long worship services that have a lot of shouting and waving of hands. Growing up in His Spirit means much more than a physical demonstration. We don't have to go to extremes to demonstrate the presence of the Holy Spirit in our lives. If we are filled with the Spirit, it will pour from within. A person who is filled with the Spirit cannot help but let it come forth because the Holy Spirit is always there.

The Holy Spirit is God contemporary.

The third reality is that the Holy Spirit is the only God that is here and now. The Holy Spirit is God contemporary. The Holy Spirit is the only real God that's here with us. He's the only on-site God. The Holy Spirit is God existential. God the Father is on the throne. God the Son is sitting at the right hand of the Father. God the Holy Spirit is here. He says, "If I don't go, he can't come." In John 14 Jesus states, "The Father and I are one." And in John 15:7 Jesus says, "If you abide in me and ... [I] abide in you, ye shall ask what you will..."

The question then becomes, "Who's here?" Is God the Father here? Is God the Son here? They are all here in the person of the Holy Spirit. But the Holy Spirit is the God on-site. Jesus is not

The Holy Spirit is the here and now God.

walking around in the flesh in the twentieth century. Jesus, the incarnate God, is not here now. The Holy Spirit is the here and now God. He's the contemporary God.

Growing up in His Spirit means realizing that the Holy Spirit is a fully-empowered, on-site, existential God.

If you don't believe that the Spirit is an on-site God, try Him. Call on Him, and see if He will not hear you. If you're having a hard time trusting, wait until your back is against the wall and you have nothing to lose. If you've got nothing to lose, give the Holy Spirit a chance. I ask you to do this because I know that the Holy Spirit will not fail you at any time—you must give Him a try! If you go around stiff-arming, not trusting and scared, you will never grow up in His Spirit. You will never live a victorious life or grow up to the Head. Growing up to the Head in His Spirit means learning to trust the Spirit.

Growing up to the Head in His Spirit means learning to trust the Spirit.

This is the fourth reality: it is God's will that you be filled. The text speaks to us about the duties of a Christian life. The context of this passage is not speaking of spiritual gifts, but rather the duties of a Christian. It begins by saying, "Be not dumb." I like the way God tries to get our attention with this. God ought to have our attention when He says, "Don't be a dummy." I like clichés and adages. I saw one on a marquee that said, "Dumb Defined: doing the same thing, and expecting different results." That is dumb! Sometimes I think about how we operate in the church—our church ministries, our church auxiliaries, our Sunday schools, our prayer meetings, our Bible studies, our choirs—we do the same things and expect different results. That's dumb! Change is necessary for a different result. But oh, how we hate change! Oh, how the flesh hates change! Some people don't even want to change their regular Sunday morning seat! We get upset if somebody sits in our seat. The flesh does not like change, but in the Christian life, change is necessary to get a different result.

God said, "Don't be dumb." I'm telling you don't be dumb in understanding the will of God in your Christian life. God

> *If you are a Christian and you are not filled with the Spirit, you are in a backsliding posture.*

said, "Be not drunk with wine, wherein is excess, but be filled with the Spirit." Some of us read that verse in a different way, such as, "*Be not drunk with wine* in excess."

Then we say, "Be filled with the Holy Spirit." We put all the emphasis on the first part of the sentence. The verb "be" is the infinitive; the verb is directed to all who receive the message; the verb is imperative present. It means "always being filled." It is directed to everyone—educated and uneducated, Black, White, rich, poor, sophisticated, unsophisticated. It's everybody—an unspecified you. It's a command. You sir ... you ma'am ... you brother ... you sister ... you preacher ... you deacon ... you trustee ... you usher ... you young person—unspecified, plural you. All of you, be filled with the Spirit!

This sentence also contains an imperative verb; it's not optional. The only option is backsliding. If you are a Christian and you are not filled with the Spirit, you are in a backsliding posture. You may not think so, but I say you are.

MANIFESTATION OF THE SPIRIT-FILLED LIFE

Everybody has an opinion about how people ought to act when they are filled with the Holy Spirit. The "how" is not the most important thing; the filling is. It doesn't matter if you shout it out or if you sit in the silence of a quiet moment. Any manifestation of how it happens is secondary to what is seen and experienced in your life. The important thing is living a victori-

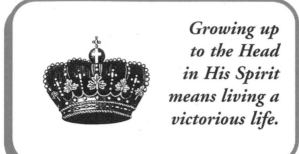

Growing up to the Head in His Spirit means living a victorious life.

ous life. Growing up to the Head in His Spirit means living a victorious life.

In this passage, we are admonished to be neither intoxicated nor unfilled. No one would tolerate a pastor coming into the pulpit drunk, trying to preach. We wouldn't tolerate a drunk deacon or a drunk trustee or a drunk usher, either. Yet, if a church leader comes to church unfilled, no one says a word. Unfilled deacons, trustees and other church leaders serve in these positions all the time, yet no one is bothered by it. Generally, when evangelical Christians read that verse, we put our emphasis on the part about drunkenness, not on the necessity to be filled with the Spirit.

The reality of the problem is this: you can't trust a person who is drunk, and you can't trust a Christian who is not filled with the Holy Spirit. Notice they are in the same category: the drunk and the unfilled Christian. God puts the wino and the unfilled Christian in the same sentence. You can't trust a drunk preacher; neither can you trust an unfilled preacher. You can't trust an unfilled preacher because he can only preach out of personal opinion, personal philosophy and personal experience. An unfilled preacher is no better than a drunk preacher because both of them are talking about something that is not of God. A drunk preacher can't discern the voice of God, and neither can an unfilled preacher.

You can't trust a drunk deacon or an unfilled deacon. According to the biblical qualifications of a deacon, he should be full of the Holy Spirit. The text said, "Look among you for seven men that are filled with the Holy Spirit" (Acts 6:3).

You can't trust a drunk trustee or an unfilled trustee. You can't trust a drunk Sunday School teacher, and you can't trust an unfilled Sunday School teacher. You can't trust an unfilled church member because he or she has the capacity to grin in your face for fifteen years, and then talk negatively about you. Growing up in His Spirit means remembering the best and forgetting the rest. You can't trust unfilled members, because they can support the church for ten years, but after one misunderstanding, they will take the church and trash it like garbage. If you're drunk with wine, or with the wine of the world, you need to step down from your leadership position. James Weldon Johnson correctly assessed this condition in "Lift E'vry Voice and Sing," when he addressed forgetting God and being drunk with the wine of the world.

BIBLICAL MODELS OF BEING FILLED WITH HIS SPIRIT

In Luke 1:15, John the Baptist was filled with the Holy Spirit, even in his mother's womb. Not only was John the Baptist filled, verse 41 said his mother, Elizabeth, was filled with the Holy Spirit. How could it be that this boy had jumped in his mother's womb? Daddy Zacharias, however, had a problem with the Holy Spirit. He was a prime example of how people can do service to the Lord yet not be filled. Daddy Zacharias held a high position in the temple, yet he stiff-armed the Holy Spirit. That's something that you can't intellectualize nor rationalize. Because Zacharias stiff-armed the Holy Spirit, God shut up his mouth and made him mute. God is a God of second chances. If you look at verse 67, old, doubting, mute Zacharias was filled with the Holy Spirit! God opened his mouth, and he began to bless the name of the Lord.

In Luke 4:1, Jesus was full of the Holy Spirit when he returned from Jordan and was led by the Spirit into the wilderness. The Book of Acts, also written by Luke, was not really the acts of the apostles, but the acts of the Holy Spirit. You take the Holy Spirit out of the Book of Acts, and it's like cutting the heart out of the body. It's like taking the sun out of the sky. In Acts 2, Peter preached and the believers present were filled with the Holy Spirit. In Acts 4:7, Peter was filled with the Holy Spirit. Stephen, that great deacon, was full of the Holy Spirit. Stephen was so great, the Bible says, that when he came home, Jesus stood up. Isn't that something? It's something to be so full of the Holy Spirit that it causes Jesus Himself to stand up when you come home to meet Him. How often does a king stand to greet a servant?

Paul, on the Damascus Road, in Acts 9:17, went down to a street called Straight Street. The Bible says that when he received his sight, he was full. How many times does God have to use His sledge hammer on us? One time ought to be enough, but sometimes He has to use it over and over again. Believe and be filled with the Holy Spirit. Growing up in His Spirit means knowing that you are in constant need of His power.

Do you know what it means to be full? Being full is like when you've gone to

> *Growing up in His Spirit means knowing that you are in constant need of His power.*

your favorite "all-you-can-eat" restaurant and you eat so much you can hardly stand up. Being full is the feeling you have after you have shared the same story with your grandson that you shared with his father when he was just a little boy. Full is the feeling you have when you see your son or daughter walk across the podium to receive his or her college degree. There

You can't be filled with the Holy Spirit and sin at the same time.

are many things that cause us to feel full. We can even be full with a feeling of guilt, but full nevertheless.

Generally, a feeling of fullness is a good feeling. Sometimes it is even good for us to be "full" with guilt—for those feelings can lead us to repentance and wholeness. However, God wants us to be full of the Holy Spirit. Being full of the Holy Spirit means there's no more room for anything else. When the Holy Spirit fills us, He consumes us. He is our protection. You know how it is when you have eaten so much that the thought of another bite of food seems repulsive? We should be so filled with the Holy Spirit that the thought of putting anything else inside our bodies is repulsive. The Holy Spirit and sin are incompatible. You can't be filled with the Holy Spirit and sin at the same time. In order to be filled with the Spirit, you have to let Him take control. The Spirit controls us; we do not control the Spirit. Growing up in His Spirit means letting the Spirit take control of you.

The good news is, even though you can't control the Holy Spirit, you can trust the Holy Spirit. The Holy Spirit is not in the hurting business. The Holy Spirit is in the helping business. The Holy Spirit does not hurt anybody. Some people say things like, "Well I don't want the Holy Spirit because I know somebody who went off the deep end dealing with the Holy Spirit." To that I

> *If you really want the Holy Spirit to take control, you've got to get desperate to be filled.*

respond, "Well, I know somebody who died in bed, but I'm still going to sleep in one tonight." Just because somebody dies in a car accident won't stop me from ever driving again. You can trust the Holy Spirit.

If you really want the Holy Spirit to take control, you've got to get desperate to be filled. You got to get sick and tired of being sick and tired. You've got to get tired of having a fever, followed by a chill. You've got to get tired of picking yourself up out of the pigpen of sin. You got to get desperate if you want to walk in the Spirit. Growing up in His Spirit requires the desperation necessary to seek Him out. We all need to be filled with the Spirit. God started the Church with a rushing wind and a fire. He didn't mean for it to end in a fizzle.

APPLICATION

Just imagine a church where everyone has decided to grow up to the Head in His Spirit! That means those who are teaching Sunday school have received the anointing. Those who are leading ministries have received the anointing. The ushers have received the anointing so that even as they greet people at the door, their Spirit-filled nature comes through. Those sitting in the pews have been blessed with the anointing so that they are filled with the Spirit as they sing praises, as they give their tithes and offerings and as they receive the Word from on High. Those who collect the offering are filled with the anointing. That can't help but be a growing church.

A Spirit-filled church is so full, it doesn't have time to gossip and condemn the teenage girl who got pregnant. A Spirit-filled church doesn't have time to talk about the couple whose son got arrested for stealing a car. A Spirit-filled church is spending its time trying to discern how to lift people up, not tear them down. A church whose

> *The Spirit-filled church will not have room for sin and destruction, but it will always have room for those seeking to be filled.*

members are dedicated to lifting up people, not tearing them down, will absolutely be a growing church. It is filled with the Spirit and will bring in others and grow them up in the Spirit as well. The Spirit-filled church will not have room for sin and destruction, but it will always have room for those seeking to be filled.

Early in the chapter, I shared some information concerning my childhood experiences and background. What I did not mention was how critical I was of the church and the preacher. Before I got saved, I despised preachers, particularly Baptist preachers. I perceived them to be womanizers and flock fleecers. Isn't it wonderful how God changes the order of our thinking once we get saved and receive the Holy Spirit? Growing up in His Spirit means having the order of our thinking changed.

Today, as a Spirit-filled Baptist preacher, I am equally critical of the Church and of Christians who sincerely don't realize the need to live Spirit-filled lives. If we really believe in the doctrine of the Trinity, we should celebrate the Day of Pentecost with as much emphasis as we do Christmas. Christmas is the time when we celebrate the arrival of the manifestation of the pre-existent Son. "And the Word was made

We spend time in preparation of everything but the Holy Spirit.

flesh [incarnate], and dwelt among us, (and we beheld his glory, the glory as of the only begotten of the Father,) full of grace and truth" (John 1:14). Why, then, on the fiftieth day after the resurrection, don't we celebrate the arrival of the manifestation of the pre-existent co-equal of the Godhead we call the Holy Spirit?

Many churches put Labor Day and Memorial Day on their calendars and ignore the Day of Pentecost. This is a clear illustration of not having grown up to the Head in His Spirit. The time between Resurrection and Pentecost is just as important as the time between Ash Wednesday and Resurrection (Lent), and the time between Thanksgiving and Christmas (Advent). We spend time preparing for everything but the Holy Spirit. This is an indication of our resistance to what God has given us. Churches and Christians that under-utilize the Holy Spirit don't grow because they can't. You simply can't grow beyond yourself without

A church with a God-sized vision must grow up to the Head in His Spirit.

growing up to the Head in His Spirit. A church with a God-sized vision must grow up to the Head in His Spirit. Christians who want to live a victorious life must grow up in His Spirit.

Christians who want to become better Christians and church members must grow up in His Spirit. Christians who want to help their churches grow numerically must grow up in His Spirit. Christians and churches who desire to carry out His last commandment, the Great Commission, must grow up in His Spirit: "Go ye therefore, and teach all nations, baptizing them in the name of the Father, and of the Son, and of the Holy Spirit: Teaching them to observe all things whatsoever I have com-

Growing up to the Head in His Spirit means learning to cooperate with His Spirit.

manded you: and, lo, I am with you alway, even unto the end of the world. Amen" (Matthew 28:19-20).

You simply cannot fulfill the Great Commission without

Acts 1:8: "But ye shall receive power, after that the Holy Ghost is come upon you: and ye shall be witnesses unto me both in Jerusalem, and in all Judaea, and in Samaria, and unto the uttermost part of the earth."

Don't be weak, foolish, unwise or dumb. It is God's will that you grow up in His Spirit: "Be ye filled." The Scriptures are our best source of instruction relative to the application of the admonishment. God tells us to be filled, then He goes on to tell us how to continuously be filled. Church members and congregations will demonstrate evidence of being filled with the Spirit. Growing up to the Head in His Spirit means learning to cooperate with His Spirit. First, cooperate with His Spirit by having a joyful relationship with Him and with each other. Ephesians 5:19 reads, "Speaking to yourselves in psalms and hymns and spiritual songs, singing and making melody in your heart to the Lord…"

Second, cooperate with His Spirit by having a grateful relationship with Him. Verse 20 tells us, "Giving thanks always for all things unto God and the Father in the name of our Lord Jesus Christ…" Growing up to the Head in His Spirit means having a grateful relationship with Him. In other words, let the whole congregation cooperate with the Spirit who lives deep down in their hearts so that the church will overflow in unison with the fullness of His presence in joyful worship. Demonstrative evidence of this will add numerically to the church in an uncontrollable manner.

Singing is a powerful channel of expression to fulfill this Christian responsibility. Congregations that have grown up to the Head in His Spirit are singing churches; singing to each other and singing directly to God with thankful hearts.

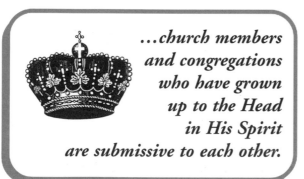

…church members and congregations who have grown up to the Head in His Spirit are submissive to each other.

Third, church members and congregations who have grown up to the Head in His Spirit are submissive to each other. Mutual submission, based upon shared reverence for Christ as Lord, is demonstrated by those who have grown up in His Spirit. Again, this is not the demonstration or manifestation of a spiritual gift. It is the responsibility of every Christian to be submissive one to the other. Compromise is not submissiveness. If you are to be submissive to one another, each party must be willing to release personal wishes for the good of all parties. Submissiveness fertilizes an environment of church growth. Submissive congregations will always be growing congregations. Growing up to the Head in His Spirit means being submissive one to the other.

Submissive congregations will always be growing congregations.

Can you imagine a church that fulfills all three of these Christian responsibilities not growing? Can you imagine how much your church will grow if you grow up to His Spirit by fulfilling all three of these Christian responsibilities? Can you imagine how much you will grow? It is your Christian responsibility to so do. Grow up to the Head in His Spirit!

FOR STUDY AND REVIEW

Chapter Eight
Growing Up to the Head in His Spirit

1. God's _____ is the guiding light for our existence. The danger lies in the desire to have the entire Christian experience begin and end in the _____.

2. Growing up to the Head in His Spirit combines both being filled with the Spirit and knowing the word of God. In which area do you need to be strengthened so that you can grow up in His Spirit? Why?

3. What is God's will for every believer? Has that will been fulfilled in you? If so, how does being filled with the Spirit manifest itself in your life?

4. What are you doing in your Christian walk that constitutes "stiff-arming" the Holy Spirit?

5. What are the four realities of being Spirit-filled?

   (a) _____

   (b) _____

   (c) _____

   (d) _____

6. What is the definition of dumb? How does that definition relate to a Christian's efforts without the empowerment of the Holy Spirit?

7. Unfilled people always look for negative things and take advantage of them. Upon what kinds of things does an unfilled person focus his or her attention?

8. The author lists two manifestations of living a Spirit-filled life. What are they?

Growing Up in His Word

Read Acts 2. What are the evidences of being filled with the Holy Spirit? What was first required of the group prior to being filled? What was the ultimate result of their being filled?

Growing Up Together

The church was born out of individuals being filled with the Spirit of God. How has the Church moved away from the very person who gave birth to her? Discuss whether the Church can survive without embracing all of the benefits of the Holy Spirit.

Growing Up to the Head!

Being filled is a continuous act. Every believer must ask God to refill him or her because of the daily leakage. Can you identify anything which causes a constant "leak in your vessel," which needs to be removed from your life? The Holy Spirit will not only refill us, but He has also empowered us to break the cycle of habitual sin that robs and causes our vessels to leak. Pray today and seek the wisdom, guidance and filling of the Holy Spirit.

GROWING UP TO THE HEAD

In Relationships

I t's sad to see a person who has grown old without ever having nurtured or developed a relationship. I believe the most important things we do in life are cen-

Submitting yourselves one to another in the fear of God.
Ephesians 5:21

tered around relationships. When we draw our last breath, all that really matters is whether we loved and were loved in return. If we don't have relationships, we really don't have anything.

In terms of spiritual growth, whether individual spiritual growth or church growth, the word relationship is second only to the word Gospel. Relationships are not just one of the critical principles of spiritual and church growth. Relationships are the essential principle. Relationships are a must for Christian growth.

Christian relationships have been explained using the horizontal and vertical directions of the cross. First, there is the vertical relationship between us and Him, the up and down relationship from heaven to earth. Then there is the horizontal relationship, the one

Growing up in relationships means being in relationships, both vertical and horizontal.

that exists among humankind. However, some Christians just want to be vertical. They want to relate to Jesus and Jesus alone. They don't want to relate to their imperfect fellow believers. Other Christians just want to be horizontal Christians. They want to socialize and hang with their Christian brothers and sisters, but don't want to have to deal with Jesus one-on-one. Horizontal relationships can be tough. Sometimes it's really hard to "love thy neighbor," even when that "neighbor" is your spouse or your child. All of us are unlovable at times. Every person has the capacity to be mean-spirited and self-seeking, which leads to hurting others. Growing up in relationships means being in relationships, both vertical and horizontal.

In Matthew 22:36-40, a young lawyer asked Jesus, "Master, which is the great commandment in the law? Jesus said unto him, Thou shalt love the Lord thy God with all thy heart, and with all thy soul, and with all thy mind. This is the first and great commandment. And the second is like unto it, Thou shalt love thy neighbour as thyself. On these two commandments hang all the law and the prophets." Jesus was saying that everything we do hangs on two commandments concerning relationships: our relationship to God and our relationship to others.

To help with horizontal relationships, we at Greenforest try to do what we call Community Time in our ministries, our auxiliaries and our committees. Instead of beginning meetings with the usual reading of the minutes or the meeting agenda, we spend about thirty minutes or more dividing ourselves into small groups, just doing Community Time. The rules are that we cannot discuss church business, politics or sports while in the groups. The purpose of the groups is to strengthen and build relationships. That is the time for us to ask one another, "How are you doing? How is your family? Did your mother get out of the hospital yet?" When we first did this in our ministerial staff meeting, we started out planning to use thirty minutes; however, when we were done, ninety minutes had passed. In the deacon's meeting we now spend at least forty-five minutes relating to each other on a personal level. We've asked our ushers and choirs and other ministries to do the same. We can get so busy doing church business that our relationships break down.

In *The Antioch Effect* (Broadman & Holman, 1994), Dr. Ken Hemphill lists six categories of relationship relative to spiritual and church growth:

1. *The first necessary relationship is between the pastor and God.* If the pastor doesn't have a relationship with God, the church is in a hurting situation.

2. *Second, the member's relationship to God is important.* The members of the church must have a relationship with God for church growth to occur.

3. *The relationship between the pastor and the members is crucial.* I've often said that, in my pastorate, I do not have any enemies, just many confused friends. One time when I said that from the pulpit, a couple of my confused friends made an appointment to see me. They admitted to me that they were confused and were dealing with something I knew nothing about. They weren't my enemies, but my confused

friends. God has blessed me to the degree that I've been delivered from pride. I'll do all that I can to make amends in a relationship.

4. *The fourth relationship is that between the members and the pastor.* There must be a desire for a relationship. Some churches have a reputation for fighting the pastor. It doesn't matter who the pastor is, they're going to fight him. There's an old joke about a pastor who accepted a call to a church with a history of ousting pastors. After his fifth year, he got really curious as to why he had survived so long when others had failed. He asked some of his deacons why the church had accepted him but not his predecessors. One deacon replied, "Well, Brother Pastor, when the preacher before you left, we got together and decided that we really didn't want a preacher or a pastor. You were the closest thing we could find." Some folks want to be in the church, but they don't want to be led.

5. *The relationship between members is essential.* The church cannot grow if the members don't like each other and won't speak to each other. There was a news brief in a Christian magazine about a choir member who threw drain cleaner on a fellow choir member because the one said the other couldn't sing. There was a serious problem between the members in that church.

6. *Finally, there must be a relationship between the church and the community.* There must be a relationship between the church and the world. There must be a relationship between the church and society. There must be a relationship between the church and missions.

UNITY

Growing up in relationships means growing up in unity. Often, when a church is in disagreement, there is a tendency for one side to want to say that the other side is "filled with the devil." Every side wants to think that God is on *their* side because they want to be right. Differences of opinion are normal and healthy among some groups of people. For some reason, in the church, we feel there can be no room for differences of opinion. There are times when each of us is wrong. Nobody is right all the time. When there is dissension within a church body, the entire group needs to be committed to praying for a solution which is guided by the Holy Spirit. Very often, however, we get caught up with sides. Everybody wants his or her side to "win." In all human relationships, when one person or group considers themselves to be the "winner," no one wins in actuality. In our relationships, both parties should strive to end dissension with harmony and to ensure that the relationship remains loving and intact. Growing up to the Head in relationships means a commitment to unity.

> *Growing up to the Head in relationships means a commitment to unity.*

The 4th Chapter of Ephesians addresses the concept of Christian unity. We know from reading the New Testament that there were plenty of disagreements within the early church, about issues such as circumcision, eating sacrificial meat, inequities and favoritism. Much of the New Testament is an account of the early church trying to figure out what it meant to be the body of Christ. After reading the first thirteen verses, it becomes easier to understand unity as a process. The early church members were people from different racial, ethnic, socio-economic and religious backgrounds, bound together by their belief in Jesus as the

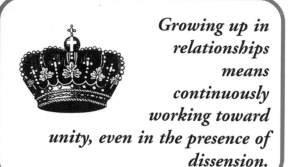

Growing up in relationships means continuously working toward unity, even in the presence of dissension.

Messiah, the Son of God. That shared belief was more important than their other differences. Their belief in Christ gave them the desire to stick together until they reached solutions to their disagreements.

The Church today, including individual local churches, is comprised of different groups of people with different backgrounds, interests and life experiences. In spite of whatever differences that exist, the contemporary church is equally bound to the bond of unity through Christ Jesus. The Book of Acts mentioned several times that the people were acting on one accord. This means they all prayed, worked, and believed together, based on "one faith, one Lord, one baptism" (Ephesians 4:5).

Our unity—our oneness—is not based on whether the church parking lot needs to be resurfaced this year or the next. In the church, any time there is a disagreement, we want to blame it on Satan. The disagreement may not be Satan's doing; but, if the situation is not resolved in Christian love, the resulting disharmony may well be Satan's handiwork. Growing up to the Head in relationships means continuously working toward unity, even in the presence of dissension.

Unity doesn't mean everybody will always agree. Many people in the church have interpreted Philippians 2:2—"Fulfil ye my joy, that ye be like-minded, having the same love, being of one accord, of one mind"—as meaning that everyone should always agree. We know that just does not happen with human beings who relate to one another on a continual basis. There is a saying about disagreements in relationships, which says that if in a relationship two people agree on everything, then one of them is unnecessary.

Sometimes the most disagreeable person in the church is right. Sometimes the most negative person in the church raises a good point to be considered. Sometimes the person who fights the pastor on everything needs to be heard. It's healthy to disagree. It is not healthy to pretend there is no room for differing opinions.

Disagreement is not always simply a black-and-white matter. It is not always a matter of right versus wrong. Sometimes two parties just disagree about how to get to the same end. For example, a person coming to visit my home will get different directions on how to get there, depending on

> *Satan gets an opening to come in when we quit speaking to someone who does not think as we do.*

whether the directions are given by me or my wife. Neither one of us is wrong. Both directions are perfectly valid. We just have a different way of defining what is easier. My wife, Sadie, thinks it's easier to get on the interstate and avoid making turns in unfamiliar territory. I think traveling the surface roads is quicker, even though there are more turns involved. Does that mean we lack unity because we prefer taking a different route to get to our home? Of course it doesn't. Sometimes, it simply may be a matter of perspective based on personal experience.

When there is dissension about a particular issue in the church or in any relationship, it does not necessarily signal the presence of Satan. But any situation where disagreement exists can prove to

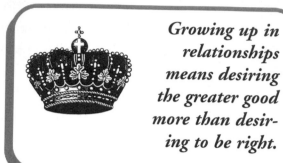

Growing up in relationships means desiring the greater good more than desiring to be right.

be fertile territory for Satan to come in, divide and conquer. Satan gets an opening to come in when we quit speaking to someone who does not think as we do. Satan gets a foot in the door to destroy relationships when there is no longer a commitment to stick together until a solution is reached. Satan enters a wide open door when we refuse to take the disagreement to a respected authority figure for a solution. The early churches sought the help of Paul and some of the other apostles. Many pastors and denominational leaders have been called in to help churches work through disagreements. Satan can only get the victory if we refuse to be open-minded or if we refuse to compromise for the greater good. Growing up in relationships means desiring the greater good more than desiring to be right.

A wise preacher once asked, "Is it better to be right, or is it better to be heard?" When a person or group is more concerned about being right, the greater cause in that relationship has been forgotten. If a pastor or church member only wants to prove that he or she is right, the unity of "one Lord, one faith, one baptism" has been forgotten. When a husband or wife simply wants to "win" the argument or disagreement and prove that he or she is "right," the oneness of the marriage has been damaged and the greater good, which is the marriage, has been forgotten. If a parent simply wants to show his or her child that "I'm grown and I'm right," or always employs the "because I said so" philosophy, the greater cause, training and guiding the child, has been cast aside for the sake of ego. Parents can have a rule that they are

To place unity of spirit as the greater good is fundamental to growing up in relationships.

always right, yet lose the love and respect of their children. A husband can maintain an attitude that "I'm the head of this house, and what I say goes," but lose the love and respect of his wife.

To place unity of spirit as the greater good is fundamental to growing up in relationships. But the commitment to unity must be valued by all parties involved. Some people, especially in one-on-one relationships, have been abused under the cause of "peace at any price." That means one party in the relationship has committed to doing whatever is necessary to avoid disharmony. Avoiding disharmony should not be confused with the commitment to resolve disharmony. Avoiding disharmony involves denial and does not promote spiritual growth. The commitment to resolve disharmony, with all its wrestling and wrangling, is a conduit to spiritual growth. There are people right now, in churches, in marriages and in families, who are still holding pain, hurt and anger because there was no commitment toward resolution. Growing up to the Head in relationships means both giving and forgiving.

GROWING UP IN MARRIAGE RELATIONSHIPS

Ephesians 5:22-33 deals primarily with the marriage relationship. Verse 21 says if you are filled with the Spirit, you will be submissive to one another. Some of us don't want to be submissive to anything or anybody. Most of the time, we want to skip past verse 21, which tells us to honor Christ by submitting to one another.

> *Mutual submission means acknowledging one another's gifts and putting egos aside so that the marital relationship can grow.*

Husbands are quick to point out that their wives are supposed to submit to them. After all, the Bible says so. But in their haste to point out the wife's failure, husbands sometimes overlook where they have fallen short. They may have fallen short in the area of mutual submission. Mutual submission means acknowledging one another's gifts and putting egos aside so that the marital relationship can grow. That means if a husband is not as knowledgeable about money management as his wife, he should not hold to a sense of false pride concerning being "in charge."

Many of us then want to read past verse 21 of Ephesians. The text, in verse 22, says for wives to submit to their husbands. On first reading, the woman of the 90's doesn't want to hear that. She chafes at the thought. But this is a self-chosen submission and cannot be forced upon her by the husband or anyone else. When done in the Spirit, it has nothing to do with superiority or inferiority. It is an equal submitting to an equal for the harmony of the marriage and the family, just as it is with Christ and the Church.

In order to understand the full meaning of verse 22, verses 21 and 23 have to be included. Verse 23 tells husbands to love their wives as much as Christ loves the church. How much did Christ love the Church? He gave his life for it. Christ loved the Church more than He loved His own body. Therefore, a Christian man should love his wife equally as much. A

Christian man does not beat himself up; nor does he verbally abuse or neglect himself. If a man will not do that to himself, he should not do that to his wife.

Conversely, a man who loves his wife more than himself should not be mistreated or disrespected by his wife. She should not attempt to take advantage of his love for her or interpret his love as weakness. In a

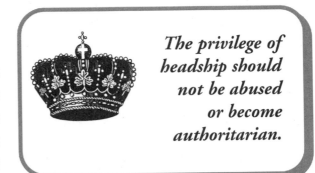

The privilege of headship should not be abused or become authoritarian.

healthy, godly marriage, both the husband and wife give one another a sacred trust. She willingly gives her submission, and he willingly lays his love at her feet. Done voluntarily, submission, is an act of supreme trust. Once a wife does this, voluntarily and without reservation, the husband must continually prove himself to be worthy of that trust.

The privilege of headship should not be abused or become authoritarian. For instance, a man may receive an opportunity to move to another city and take a job that appeals to him. His wife, however, may have strong reservations. Should the man make the decision to pack up his family and move, simply because he has spoken as head of his family? Should he ignore the desires of his wife? If the man does this, he may find that, once the move is complete, it's very lonely at the top. The move may have occurred just as the husband desired, but he has alienated his family in the process. Then what has he gained? Has he gained the love and respect of his family if he has demonstrated that he is only concerned for his own needs? A man may have to

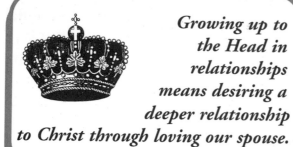

Growing up to the Head in relationships means desiring a deeper relationship to Christ through loving our spouse.

make a few mistakes like that before he starts to realize the true meaning of headship.

Perhaps one of the most glossed-over understandings concerning marriage is the process of becoming (Matthew 19:5). It is both being and becoming at the same time. When two people get married they are one, yet they are perpetually in a process of becoming one. In other words, the oneness should grow with time. From the moment the couple says "I do," they should be always striving for oneness; not to become the same person, but to grow in such a way that both become closer to Christ as a result of their relationship to one another. Growing up to the Head in relationships means desiring a deeper relationship to Christ through loving our spouse.

A man and a woman who would be married are charged to cleave to each other. Cleave means stick together like glue. It is said first in Genesis that we are to leave parents and family and cleave to each other. The reason so many marriages go down the drain is because we have too many men who are still mama's boys and too many women who are still daddy's little girl. Every time something happens, the wife wants to run back to daddy. The husband cannot give his wife a fair chance because he is always comparing her to his mother. Mama's Boy and Daddy's Girl have no business trying to marry unless they are willing to leave Mama and Daddy. The best thing parents and sisters and brothers can do is stay out of it.

GROWING UP IN FAMILY RELATIONSHIP

Much has been said in recent years about dysfunctional families, with accompanying terms like adult children. All of this terminology and the commitment to resolve the past are rooted in relationships. An entire movement is dedicated to the internal resolution of issues which could not be resolved within a relationship.

It has wisely been noted that our understanding of God results, in large part, from our relationship with our parents or primary caregiver. If the person responsible for our primary care proved trustworthy in their duty to meet our basic needs

People who grow up in neglect sometimes have a difficult time trusting God as Provider.

(physical needs, affirmation, love), then we can easily translate that trust to God. People who grow up in neglect sometimes have a difficult time trusting God as Provider. People who grow up with an abusive father sometimes have difficulty accepting belief in God as a Father who gives unconditional love.

Ephesians 6:1-4 deals with the obligations of both parents and children to maintain family harmony. Children are reminded to obey their parents, but parents are reminded to carry themselves in a manner worthy of being obeyed. Family relationships are crucial to our ability to grow up to the Head. How can a preacher accept the authority to share God's Word from the pulpit yet ignore the role of provider and caregiver in the home? How can a deacon visit a hurting church member while ignoring a hurting family member at home? It is our commitment to unity in our primary relationships that yield over to our relationships in

Family relationships are crucial to our ability to grow up to the Head.

the church. How can a pastor preach to his wife when she knows he has been unfaithful to her? How can a youth minister prepare young people for adulthood when her own daughter barely speaks to her? The sad truth is, such relationships happen all the time within our churches.

One pastor I know told about an argument he had with his wife on a Wednesday evening. As he left his wife sitting in their bedroom crying, he yelled, "I've got to get to church. I don't have time to fool with what you're talking about!" As he drove to the church, he realized that he could in no way go and attempt to minister to the congregation while his wife was at home in tears. Realizing this, he turned the car around and headed home. He and his wife did not resolve the issue at that moment; however, he had acknowledged his responsibility first as a husband. He realized that he could not be loving toward his congregation if he failed to be loving toward his wife. By storming out of the house, he felt his pastoral authority had diminished. By returning home, he made the issue of conflict less important than his relationship with his wife and the stability of his family. Growing up in relationships means having a commitment to resolve conflict by placing personal interests aside. Growing up to the Head in relationships means putting Christian duties before secular responsibilities.

GROWING UP IN PROFESSIONAL RELATIONSHIPS

Verses 5-9 in the 6th Chapter of Ephesians addresses the relationship of slave to master, or what may properly be interpreted to modern-day work relationships. "Servants, be obedient to them that are your masters according to the flesh, with fear and trembling, in singleness of your heart, as unto Christ; Not with eyeservice, as menpleasers; but as the servants of Christ, doing the will of God from the heart; With good will doing service, as to the Lord, and not to men: Knowing that whatsoever good thing any man doeth, the same shall he receive of the Lord, whether he be bond or free. And, ye masters, do the same things unto them, forbearing threatening: knowing that your Master also is in heaven; neither is there respect of persons with him."

> *Growing up in relationships means having a commitment to resolve conflict by placing personal interests aside.*

Again, the mutuality of healthy relationships is emphasized. Not only must the subordinate yield to the one in authority, but the person holding that authority must not abuse the privilege. People often quit jobs because they don't want to follow orders or submit to the authority of another. Conversely, some people abuse their authority by taking an "I'm the boss so you must do what I say" attitude. Each party is called upon to exhibit the spirit of Christ in relating to one another.

Some of you might be asking, "What if I work in an environment where I'm the only Christian?" That is the perfect environment to show the love of Christ. Those who work in environments where religion is suppressed or frowned upon have been given a great blessing. It's easy to be loving and caring toward those who demonstrate love, care and concern toward you. Growing up in relationships means showing the love of Christ to those who do not know of His love. If you do this, you will find that, over time, people will see you differently. They will want to be around you because you are pleasant to work with. Some may even come seeking advice on how to handle a problem. At that point, you have gained an opening to begin sharing Jesus with them. Sharing the love of Christ in your actions is stronger than any religious icon or symbol displayed in the workplace. Sharing the love of Christ sets you apart, sanctifies you, without the need for outward symbols.

We are reminded in Ephesians 6:8 that whatever good thing we do, no matter who we are, will be returned to us. In other words, how we treat others matters. When we go about our jobs wanting to be good stewards of the talent(s) He has given us, issues of power and authority tend to diminish. Ephesians advises Christians to do our work as though we are working for the Lord, not for someone else, willingly. By doing so, we will, in turn, receive the good we have done with the work we have been given. Those in authority over us are only in authority as far as the job is concerned. How we choose to react to that authority depends upon us.

In his book, *Man's Search for Meaning* (Beacon Press, 1992), Viktor E. Frankl talks about his experiences as a prisoner in a German concentration camp. He noticed there were some prisoners who held a different attitude. They encouraged fellow captives and even gave away their last piece of bread. From this experience, Frankl determined that the only thing that cannot be taken away is a person's ability to choose how he or she will react to his or her circumstances. Christ in us gives us the choice to combat hostility with love; to combat authoritarianism with love; to combat racism with love; to combat sexism with love; to combat petty jealousies with love. Growing up in relationships includes how we interact with those who are not in Christ, learning to love those who do not hold His love as the standard.

> *Growing up in relationships includes how we interact with those who are not in Christ ... those who do not hold His love as the standard.*

APPLICATION

Jesus gives two models for handling division in relationships. He addresses division in Matthew 5:23-24 and in Matthew 18:15-17. In the 5th Chapter of Matthew, Jesus says, "Therefore if thou bring thy gift to the altar, and there rememberest that thy brother hath aught against thee; Leave there thy gift before the altar, and go thy way; first be reconciled to thy brother, and then come and offer thy gift." If we are at odds with someone, we should first attempt to mend the broken relationship before we leave our offerings at the altar. If a father and son have had an argument, can either one make an offering to the Lord before reconciliation? What would give God greater joy and glory: money given by hands attached to a broken heart or reunion that occurs when a broken relationship is mended? We must remember that our money, our offerings, even our Christian service, in and of itself, mean nothing to God. The meaning behind what we give is what is important. It is futile for us to try to maintain a right relationship with God through worship and giving if we are not at peace with others.

A collection of Jewish teachings known as the *Mishnah* says this concerning relationships: "The day of Atonement atones for offenses of man against God, but it does not atone for offenses against man's neighbor, until he reconciles his neighbor." Sometimes we want to make "church work" or church activity more important than relationships. In this passage, Jesus is telling us that it is better to leave the church at the most sacred moment of worship rather than delay reconciliation of a broken relationship.

In Matthew 18:15-17, Jesus addresses how to handle conflict when someone has done wrong against you: "Moreover if thy brother shall trespass against thee, go and tell him his fault between thee and him alone: if he shall hear thee, thou hast gained thy brother. But if he will not hear thee, then take with thee one or two more, that in the

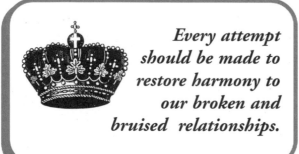

Every attempt should be made to restore harmony to our broken and bruised relationships.

mouth of two or three witnesses every word may be established. And if he shall neglect to hear them, tell it unto the church: but if he neglect to hear the church, let him be unto thee as an heathen man and a publican."

Every attempt should be made to restore harmony to our broken and bruised relationships. Basically, Jesus said it doesn't matter whether you were the one who was wronged or whether you were in the wrong. Jesus places the burden for restoring relationships on the believer. Too often, we sit around waiting for the person who wronged us to come and apologize. Family members have gone for years without speaking because of a disagreement, one waiting on the other to admit that he or she was wrong. Sometimes relationships remain broken because one or both parties are too proud to say, "I'm sorry."

Growing up in relationships means casting out pride in order for restoration to occur. Very often, the Christian mandate for conflict resolution is ignored because everyone is

> *How well a church manages conflict is a major determining factor in numerical church growth.*

out to prove right and wrong. It's very easy to get side-tracked on that issue.

It is not surprising that those who are the most disagreeable church members usually have poor marital and family relationships. They often come to the church to vent the frustrations they feel they cannot vent at home. They come to business meetings to fight. They find a reason to criticize every new ministry the church initiates. They fight with the pastor. They seek out other unhappy persons in the church to form alliances. Dealing with such people in the church takes the commitment of the church to task. A church's ability to deal with conflict and dissension is a reflection upon how far that church has grown up to the Head in relationships. Churches with immature relationships within the body will have lingering, interminable conflict.

How well a church manages conflict is a major determining factor in numerical church growth. Often, churches split because they cannot effectively resolve conflict. It is easier for them to just go their separate ways. Jesus has not called us to do what is easy. Our faith compels us to unite in spite of obstacles, not separate because of them. Churches that have grown up to the Head in relationships will meet conflict as a positive challenge, having a commitment to resolution and restoration.

In every town there are certain churches that have a reputation for being "hellraisers." They are known for the disharmony that exists within them. These are usually

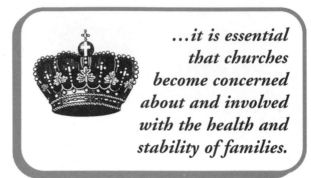

...it is essential that churches become concerned about and involved with the health and stability of families.

not growing churches. Not many people knowingly align themselves with a congregation that knows only misery, anger and alienation. For that reason, it is essential that churches become concerned about and involved with the health and stability of families. In the age of soaring divorce rates, couples need help on how to be loving toward one another. Nearly every parent struggles with their parenting skills at some point in their child's development.

People need help balancing family time with work and other demands. Christians need help with their daughters who get pregnant and with the sons who impregnate them. Christians need help without judgement when their children come home and tell them, "I'm in trouble." Christians need help to deal with their grown children who are still living at home or with aging parents who have moved in with them. A church that gains a reputation for genuine concern for its members and ministers to those concerns will be a growing church. Far too many churches are long on guilt and judgement and short on mercy and nurture.

A church that has grown up in relationships knows that life happens and that no person is excluded from its twists of fate. Every person who accepts a job risks forced termination or lay-off. Every person who marries risks divorce. Every person who has a child risks that child one day telling him or her, "I'm on drugs ... I'm gay ... I'm pregnant." In her book, *Stick a Geranium in Your Hat and Be Happy* (Inspirational Press, 1990), Barbara Johnson shares openly and intimately about her family's struggle to continue in relationship with one son after he confessed his homosexual lifestyle to them. Restoration of the rela-

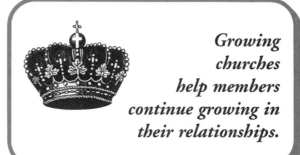

Growing churches help members continue growing in their relationships.

tionship did not happen overnight, and there were times when both the parents and the son were resistant to dialog. Neither side was willing to change or compromise. In her book, she shares how that painful period was also a growing period which later spawned many, many other ministry opportunities.

The only way to avoid the pitfalls of life is to avoid living. Growing churches help members prepare for and cope with life and its varying joys and disappointments. Growing churches help members continue growing in their relationships. A loving church can easily become a growing church, primarily because people come to the church seeking love, acceptance and understanding. A church must grow up in relationships to be able to love and nurture both its members and those seeking refuge in His love.

Very often churches, particularly evangelical churches, focus on behavior rather than the inner being. It is easier to give a list of do's and do not's. That is black-and-white Christianity, which makes life simple for the church, for the pastor and for the members. The problem with black-and-white Christianity is that it has no remedy or resolution for conflict, for tragedy or for human failure. When the inner being is grown up to Him in relationship, the outer behavior takes care of itself. Members who have grown up in their relationship to Him and to significant others help create and foster an environment suited for church growth.

FOR STUDY AND REVIEW

Chapter Nine
Growing Up to the Head in Relationships

1. In terms of spiritual growth, whether individual spiritual growth or church growth, the word _____ is second only to the word _____.

2. What does it mean to be in relationship both horizontally and vertically?

3. List the six categories of relationships relative to spiritual and church growth Dr. Ken Hemphill discusses in his book, *The Antioch Effect* (Broadman & Holman Publishers, 1994).

    (1) _____

    (2) _____

    (3) _____

    (4) _____

    (5) _____

    (6) _____

4. There are times in a relationship when each party may be wrong. During those times, each party must strive to end _____ with harmony and maintain _____.

5. Check all that are correct.

    ___ Unity requires both parties working together.

    ___ Unity means everybody always agrees.

    ___ One should avoid disharmony in order to maintain unity.

    ___ Unity requires forgiving, not giving.

6. List four primary relationships a Christian's walk can be manifested through:

    (a) _____

    (b) _____

    (c) _____

    (d) _____

7. In a marriage relationship, egos must be put aside and mutual _____ exhibited through acknowledging one another's _____.

8. Headship is a _____ which should not be abused.

9. Those who work in an environment where religion is suppressed or frowned upon have been given a great blessing. *(check one)* ____ True ____ False

Growing Up in His Word

Read Ephesians 5:21-33. What does it mean to be submissive one to another? Who is the husband's model of submission? Who is the wife's model of submission? How can a husband and wife better understand their relationship with each other? Why is a Spirit-filled life necessary to maintain unity in the relationship and help both parties grow up to the Head individually?

Growing Up Together

Think of a time when there was disagreement within your church body. Did the congregation maintain unity even though there was disagreement? What actions were taken to resolve the conflict? Did the actions reflect a congregation growing up to the Head in relationships?

Growing Up to the Head!

In order for relationships to be healthy, there must be balance between our horizontal and vertical relationships. Examine your own personal relationships as well as your relationship with God. List any relationships which may cause an imbalance and a personal action plan which will help you continue to grow up to the Head.

GROWING UP TO THE HEAD

In His Strength

A round 1975, a book by a man named John Malloy became very popular among those in the corporate work environment. The book was entitled *Dress for Success*.

Finally, my brethren, be strong in the Lord, and in the power of his might. **Ephesians 6:10**

In this book Malloy talked about the best color suit to wear, including the tie style that is expected for one who is moving up the corporate ladder. This led to the phenomena of what we call the "power" blue suit and the red "power tie" that goes along with it. Anytime the boss comes in wearing his power blue suit and red tie, you know that something is up.

I think our expectations and behavior are often determined by the way we dress. We dress down when we want to be in a relaxed mode, and we dress up to become more formal. We become more formal in our thinking and our actions when we are dressed up. As a matter of a fact, the old folks used to tell us, "I hope you act as nice as you look." I think we had a way of doing that. Somehow, when we're dressed up, we tend to act better. Also, the occasion itself often determines the way we dress. We dress casually to play; we dress formally to dine. We dress in our

How do you dress to have a spiritually victorious life?

shorts and our warm-ups to play tennis and do aerobics. We dress in helmets and shoulder pads to play ice hockey and football. How do you dress for spiritual success? How do you dress if you want to have the success of an abundant life that Jesus has brought us? How do you dress to have a spiritually victorious life? How do you dress to have the fulfilling life that Christ has promised us? What spiritual clothing should we wear? The con-

cluding chapter of the Book of Ephesians gives believers instructions on how to dress for spiritual success. Growing up to the Head in His strength means dressing for spiritual success.

Growing up to the Head in His strength means dressing for spiritual success.

Ephesians 6 is the spiritual book for Christians wanting to dress for success. Christians need to power dress, too. We have been given our own "power" suit to wear. The good news is our "power" suit doesn't cost any money. It doesn't have to be taken to the dry cleaners. It doesn't wear out. The power suit we have been given is eternal. Ephesians 6:10 tells us, "Be strong in the

> *Growing up to the Head in His strength means relying on His strength and not our own.*

Lord, and in the power of his might." That means be strong in God's power, and not in our own. Growing up to the Head in His strength means relying on His strength.

DRESS FOR SPIRITUAL SUCCESS

Chapter 6 of the Book of Ephesians deals with the Church as a soldier. We are called to be Christian soldiers in God's army. If you are going to be a soldier, you have to dress like a soldier. If you are going to be successful in spiritual warfare, you've got to dress up like a soldier who is going to war. Any soldier who goes into the battlefield unprepared for combat will be defeated.

As Christian soldiers, we must dress as if we expect to win or to have success. If we don't dress for success, we will not experience the abundant life and the joy that Christ has given us. We will not experience the power of deliverance unless we dress for spiritual success. We will not live with confidence and assurance of eternal life. We will not speak boldly about the love and the goodness of Christ as we ought. People come to Christ because they are already feeling defeated. Where is the victory in Jesus if His followers are living defeated lives?

Paul says in verse 20 "that therein that I might speak boldly as I ought to speak." Herein lies the challenge of every church member: that we will speak boldly for Christ. If you are not speaking boldly, as you ought to speak, you may not be dressed right. If you haven't told anyone lately about the love of Jesus, you just may not be dressed right. If the people on your job, who you've been with Monday through Friday, don't even know you are a Christian, you certainly aren't dressed right. If you haven't led anybody to Christ within the last year, you just may not be dressed right. If you haven't told anybody about the saving knowledge of Christ lately, you just may not be dressed right. If you haven't told somebody about the goodness of God, how and when He saved you and how He blessed you, you are not dressed right. You are not speaking boldly, as you ought to speak.

If you haven't told somebody about the goodness of God ... you are not dressed right.

Too often, we find ourselves at church, looking very lovely in our physical appearance, yet our spiritual attire is "bargain basement." We know how to dress appropriately for church, we probably know how to dress for corporate America. But the real question is, "Are we dressed to speak boldly, as we ought, to do the purpose of the Church?" The Scripture tells us how we ought to dress for spiritual success so we might speak boldly as we ought.

A look at verses 10-20 gives us the proper apparel for spiritual warfare. If you watch the news, every so often there will be a segment about the latest fashions for the new season. We can look at these verses as the new fall or spring line of clothing. The old line, the Law, is out-of-style now. You know what it feels like to wear something that is no longer in fashion. You look out of place. You stand out in a crowd, but not in a positive way. Law is the old style. The new line of clothing includes mercy and grace. In the secular fashion world, we're always being told things like whether dresses are long or short and whether lapels are narrow or wide. If your wardrobe includes some legalism, then you're out of style spiritually.

APPAREL FOR SPIRITUAL WARFARE

Growing up in His strength means being prepared for spiritual warfare. If we are to have the victory in spiritual warfare, the first thing Ephesians 6 tells us is that we ought to put on the whole armor. We are not to leave a piece off. The emphasis is on "whole." We cannot be half-dressed for warfare and expect to win.

Growing up in His strength means being prepared for spiritual warfare.

We can walk around the house half dressed, but that's not the battlefield. If we are going to win the war, we need to wear the whole armor of God. We can look at the "of God" portion as a designer label. In the fashion world, some labels represent quality better than others. If I buy a suit made by Christian Dior or Giorgio Armani, I'm reasonably assured of the quality of the garment. If I buy a suit by a designer I've never heard of before, I can't be sure that the seam won't rip when I raise my arm. That's the same kind of assurance we have when we put on the whole armor of God. We're supposed to wear armor made by God. If we put on armor made by someone else, we will be in trouble when trying to do spiritual warfare. You can't use the armor of "dead presidents" to do spiritual warfare. You can't rely on apparel designed by Yves Saint Laurent to protect you in spiritual battle. The reason we need armor designed by God is because we wrestle not with flesh and blood, but with

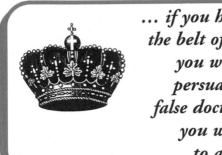

... if you have on the belt of truth, you won't be persuaded by false doctrine— you won't go to and fro.

principalities. We wrestle with rulers of darkness and spiritual wickedness in high places, not low places. Growing up to His strength means wearing armor designed by God.

Check the label of your spiritual armor. If it doesn't carry a label in it that says, "The Most High" or "Exclusively by Jehovah," "Designs by God" or "Designs of God," you're headed for spiritual defeat.

THE BELT OF TRUTH

We need to put on our belt called the belt of truth. Everybody knows that a belt is used to keep your pants up and keep your shirt from hanging out. The belt of truth is also used to keep us from flapping from one thing or another. Many Christians are just going from one doctrine to another. If you have on the belt of truth, however, you won't be persuaded by false doctrine—you won't go to and fro.

It has often concerned me to hear some of my co-pastors tell their listeners about prosperity doctrine. Some of the doctrine coming from our televangelists and pastors—I call them co-pastors—who appear on television is unbelievable. Just because a man has on a double-breasted suit and walks around with a Bible in his hand doesn't mean he knows what he's talking about. Some of our people are being co-pastored by televangelists because they listen to these preachers as much as their own pastor. They still need to put their belts on. There is no "belt of truth criterion" necessary for getting on television. No doctrinal screen-

... the belt of truth gives the Christian strength and support in times of trial and tribulation.

ing is required. Most television stations run a disclaimer that says the views of the televangelist do not necessarily represent the viewpoint of the station or its owners. Preachers pay to get on television. If you've got money, you can be on television saying just about whatever you want. Television does not validate truth. Many preachers on television have a loose belt of truth so that they can mold and shape doctrine to what is popular or to what is convenient. This is not true of all television evangelists, and, of course, non-television preachers can be equally guilty of this.

The belt of truth should be worn tightly as it keeps us from flopping around aimlessly, here and there, with no direction. The 1st Chapter of the Book of James warns us about people who are double-minded (flopping around): "But let him ask in faith, nothing wavering. For he that wavereth is like a wave of the sea driven with the wind and tossed. For let not that man think that he shall receive any thing of the Lord. A double minded man is unstable in all his ways."

A soldier's belt also gives his body strength and support. Likewise, the belt of truth gives the Christian strength and support in times of trial and tribulation. Believers experiencing trials and tribulation need to tighten their belts. Believers having adversity might need to tighten their belts. Sometimes when we've eaten too much at the dinner table, we have to loosen our belt. But one thing is for sure, if you keep that tight belt on, it will keep you from taking in more than you should. If you find yourself taking in too much of the world's confusion and uncer-

When the belt of truth is tied tightly around us, there is little room for Satan's lies to dwell inside us.

tainty, you need to tighten the belt of truth around your waist. When the belt of truth is tied tightly around us, there is little room for Satan's lies to dwell inside us.

What is this belt of truth? Christ is truth, the Word is truth. John 17:17 says, "Sanctify them through thy truth: thy word is truth." Jesus says, "I am the way, the truth, and the life: no man cometh unto the Father, but by me" (John 14:6). To dress for success, we must put on the belt of truth, and wear that belt tightly, almost like a truss, binding us to His truth. Sometimes the discomfort of a tight belt helps us to stay in focus. When the belt that holds up our pants gets too tight, we

Growing up in His strength means wearing the belt of truth tightly around us.

know it's time to take action. We eat less and we exercise. We take a corrective action because we know things are getting out of hand. Wearing the belt of truth tightly around us is for our security, not for our discomfort. A loose belt doesn't really make us feel secure. If I have on a pair of pants and the belt is loose, I cannot feel secure for fear that I may lose my pants. I want to walk with confidence. Growing up in His strength means wearing the belt of truth tightly around us. By doing so, we will feel more secure in His strength.

BREASTPLATE OF RIGHTEOUSNESS

Our wardrobe is not complete until we put on at least five other pieces of spiritual clothing. The accessory needed is the breastplate of righteousness. I do not use the term accessory in order to minimize the role of the armor of God. But accessories, just like our clothing, make the difference. You can have on a nice suit, but if the tie or the shirt or the belt or the shoes are not coordinated, the beauty of the suit is lost. Women are especially sensitive to the importance of accessories. They have to have just the right earrings, the right necklace, or the right scarf to make their outfits complete. Likewise, the proper spiritual accessories prepare us to do His work. We can be Christians, yet still be defeated in spiritual warfare because we have not donned the accessories we need for battle.

The breastplate covers the body from the neck to the thighs. It covers the internal parts, the soul, the very essence of who we are. The breastplate covers the heart. The believer is justified in his belief, in and through the heart. We need to protect our hearts. Just like the American Heart Association is constantly telling us to be "heart smart" for our health, we need to be spiritually heart smart. The breastplate of righteousness keeps the heart from being fatally wounded. The breastplate keeps us from losing heart. We can lose heart in a number of ways. Even though our faith has made us righteous and we are called to walk a righteous life, we can still lose heart. A believer who is willfully doing something wrong is about to lose heart. A Christian involved in a relationship that is wrong is about to lose heart because the heart is not protected. A believer being disobedient to the will of God in and through tithes and offerings is about

Heartache is worse than a headache, a backache or any muscle ache.

to lose heart because he or she is not protected. Believers stuffed up with pride, and thinking themselves to be "somebody," are about to lose heart. In all these cases, the one who is about to lose heart needs to put on the breastplate of righteousness. The heart needs protection so that it will not be hurt. There is no greater ache than that which comes from heartache or a broken heart. Heartache is worse than a headache, a backache or any muscle ache. The heart is life's pumping organ. The breastplate protects the pump.

SHOES OF PREPARATION

The third article that God gives us is the sandals, which are the Gospel of peace. Shoes are a sign of readiness. For example, imagine you and your family are getting ready to leave the house to go to church. All of a sudden somebody announces he or she can't find his or her shoes. That means that person isn't ready to go. Some of us who grew up in the country got accustomed to running around in bare feet; however, you were not really ready to go anywhere important until you got your shoes on. The Gospel tells us that we need to be ready. We need to put on our shoes. Don't dare go to war without shoes! I am talking about a soldier's shoes—ones with cleats.

There is a difference between shoes for dancing and shoes for battle. Dancing shoes have slick bottoms. But when we are going to do battle, we need some grip, something to give us a foothold. We need to have some leverage. We need to put on shoes with cleats or grips. It is very interesting how the secular, commercial world has picked up on what God said so long ago. Nike invented Air Jordans. They put a little cushion in the bottom to make people feel lighter. People buy Air Jordans, popularized by basketball superstar Michael Jordan, because they think it will help them increase their hang

> *Jesus is the light of the world and when we hang with Him, we will light up.*

time. We don't have to be like Mike. We need to be like Jesus. The shoes I'm talking about are not Air Jordans. I'm talking about "Air Jesus." His shoes increase our "hang time." Jesus is the light of the world and when we hang with Him, we will light up. David called them hinds' feet. David said, "You've made my feet to be like hinds' [deer] feet." God has given animals like deer and mountain goats special feet. He put suction under their feet, and inserted claws that can come out or go down, and suck up or either stay out. They are, therefore, able to jump from one place to another, stand on ice, or stand on the edge of a rock. They can defy gravity, and they can jump here and there. The devil can't do you any harm when you have hinds' feet.

SHIELD OF FAITH

There is a fourth article of clothing, and that is the shield of faith. This shield is not a small shield, as some would think, to block the darts of the devil. But this shield is something that a soldier would wear. It is a long shield. It is an oblong sturdy device that covers the whole body, protecting it from the fiery darts of doubt. Doubt is the opposite of faith. Doubt can mess us up. A fellow pastor told me about a man who came to see him one day. The man came into his office just to sit down and talk to him to be assured that he wasn't crazy. The man was beginning to doubt his sanity. His motivation for work was to increase the ministry of the church, so he worked hard. He reasoned that the more money he made, the more he could give to the ministry of that church. People were beginning to tell him he was crazy. He wanted the pastor to pinch him and make sure that he wasn't crazy.

Sometimes the devil can just mess us up so badly that we think we are crazy. People in the world can tell believers that we are crazy for doing some of the things we do. A preacher came down the isle of our church one day with tears in his eyes. He told me, "I am so thankful for this church, because I thought I was crazy. I've pastored two churches and I am not pastoring any more. I wasn't even going to church because people made me think I was crazy. They convinced me that my vision for the church was crazy. But now that I'm here at Greenforest, I know I'm not crazy. Thank God, I'm not crazy!"

Sometimes we can doubt so much that we think we are crazy! People can cause us to doubt. The fiery darts of the devil can cause us to doubt. I remember hearing about a study that was done of children who had been misdiagnosed and wrongly admitted to an institution for children who had mental handicaps. The study showed that, even though the children were of normal intelligence, they began to act as though they were mentally retarded. The children discovered that acting "normal" in an institution for the mentally retarded got them in trouble. For their survival, they began to act as though they were mentally challenged. Sometimes we can be placed in an environment where we feel we have to be someone other than who we are in order to survive. The insanity of the world can cause us to doubt even our salvation. It can cause us to begin to doubt the goodness of God.

> *Growing up in His strength means learning to shield ourselves from the flaming darts of evil, which cause us to doubt Him.*

Growing up in His strength means learning to shield ourselves from the flaming darts of evil, which cause us to doubt Him. When adversity comes upon us, and we know that we've been trying to live a good life, we may doubt. We begin to doubt because ... my child is in trouble ... my husband died ... I lost my job. These kinds of trauma cause us to begin to doubt. Doubt will cause confusion and mess us up. That is why we need to put on the shield of faith.

The shield must be put on every morning. Many years ago, the manufacturers of Right Guard® deodorant spoke a lot about the necessity of protection from odor. They promoted Right Guard® as a shield of protection. Just like you don't leave your house without your deodorant, don't leave home without your shield of faith. If you leave home without underarm deodorant, you will realize it before too long. If you leave home without the shield of faith, you will certainly know that before too long. Don't let this world catch you with your shield of faith down. As American Express® says, "Don't leave home without it."

Growing up in His strength means knowing that the shield of faith is our protection. To use a phrase from the 1960's, "Keep the faith." We must keep the faith in all things. We must be like Jesus and tell Satan, "Get thee behind me, Satan" (Mark 8:33; Luke 4:8). When we are dressed for success, we have on the shield of faith so that the fiery darts of evil just bounce off.

HELMET OF SALVATION

The helmet of salvation, the fifth garment, covers the head and the mind. Jesus healed a lunatic, a man called Legion, who was cutting himself in the graveyard (Mark 5:1-15). This man didn't even know his real name but called himself Legion because there were so many demons inside of him. He came to Jesus. Jesus cast the devils out of him and put them into a herd of pigs. Then Jesus made the pigs go drown themselves in the sea. The Bible says that when the people from town came, the man was sitting up, clothed in his right mind. The people were frightened. They were not able to rejoice in this man's salvation. Why couldn't they rejoice? Were they more concerned about the loss of their pigs? You know he must have gotten saved if he was clothed and in his right mind. I'm not too sure we aren't the same today. With our love for materialism, we can shout on materialism but can't give a word of praise for God when He saves someone.

We need the helmet of salvation to protect the mind. The Bible says, "... be ye not conformed to this world, but be ye transformed by the renewing of your mind" (Romans 12:2). When we get saved we think about things differently. An unsaved man sees nothing wrong with being his own man and making choices as he sees fit.

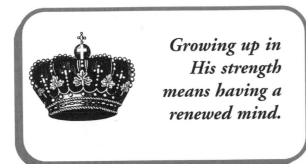

Growing up in His strength means having a renewed mind.

An unsaved woman sees nothing wrong with trying to do her own thing according to her own knowledge. An unsaved mind cannot resist temptation, because that mind has yet to be renewed. Growing up in His strength means having a renewed mind. A renewed mind relies on faith, not on human reason or thinking. An unsaved mind thinks the mind is sufficient to meet the challenges of the day. A renewed mind puts the burden for meeting the day's challenges upon faith. We need a renewed mind in order to be saved.

SWORD OF THE SPIRIT

The final piece of equipment which completes the armor of God is the sword of the Spirit, which is the Word of God. A Christian is naked without the Word of God. Being naked is not being dressed for spiritual success. A Christian is not appropriately dressed without the Word.

In Psalm 119:11, the psalmist tells us the importance of God's word to us: "Thy word have I hid in mine heart, that I might not sin against thee." We need the Word in order to do spiritual battle. The word is the only offensive weapon in the collection which makes up the full armor of God. Everything else is a piece of equipment designed for defense. The word is a two-edge sword. Hebrews 4:12 tells us, "For the word of God is quick, and powerful, and sharper than any twoedged sword, piercing even to the dividing asunder of soul and spirit, and of the joints and marrow, and is a discerner of the thoughts and intents of the heart."

A double-edge sword cuts two ways. It cuts to comfort those who need comforting, but it also cuts to disturb those who need disturbing. Some people come to church in need of a word of comfort. Others who come need a word of conviction and a word of disturbance.

The prophet Amos said, "You're in trouble because you're too much at ease in Zion" (Amos 6:1). His prophetic words are still true today. God's people have gotten too comfortable in the church, doing church their own way. People need disturbing sometimes; therefore, the word cuts both ways. That's a powerful weapon! Imagine a weapon which can both heal the wounded and cut the enemy.

THE PROBLEM OF "DRESSING DOWN"

The word of God tells us to put on the whole armor of God. But why don't we? We know what the word of God says, yet we don't put on the whole armor of God. I believe our problem is that often, we dress down for war. We "dress down" too soon. Dressing down is popular today. In Corporate America they have "dress down" day or "corporate casual" day. Even in our church's academy, where the children wear uniforms, every once in a while we have "dress down" day. Many times it is good to relax, dress down and get comfortable. There is a warning, however, that you don't need to dress down too fast. This game of spiritual warfare is played from the cradle to the grave. A lot of teams lose in the fourth quarter. A lot of teams lose in the last sixty seconds of the game. We have to run this race all the way in order to have the victory—so don't dress down! Growing up to His strength means learning not to dress down.

Growing up to His strength means learning not to dress down.

A leader in our church once told me about something that happened to him in corporate America. He was a high-level executive at the time with a large company. One day the company was having a meeting in a fancy hotel, and the boss said they were going to dress down. So he, like all the other executives, dressed down. He went down for breakfast and a lady walked up to him and said, "Boy, will you get my bags for me?" To her, the only difference

between an execu-
tive and the boy who
was going to carry
her bags to her room
was the way he was
dressed. Don't dress
down too quickly in
battle. Don't play

**Don't let
Satan steal
your peace and
your hope!**

the devil cheap. Don't underestimate the enemy. We may be still
on the battlefield, but he is still on the battlefield, too. God is real,
but so is the devil. Jesus is the Prince of Peace, and the devil is the
prince of this world. Don't dress down!

Revelation 16:15 says, "Behold I come as a thief. Blessed is he
that watcheth [watch and pray], and keepeth his garments, lest
he walk naked, and they see his shame." We need to be on guard
at all times. Don't let the devil steal your joy! Don't let the evil
one steal your love! Don't let Satan steal your peace and your
hope!

Dressed for Prayer

Whatever you do, Ephesians 6:18 says don't dress down in
prayer. Verse 18 says dress up in prayer. The devil will steal your
spiritual clothing if you don't dress up in prayer. It says that we
ought to be praying in the Spirit always. Dress up when it's time
to pray. Dress up in the Spirit, and pray in the Spirit. Dress up
and pray for everybody because this is not a solo thing. Church
prayer is a common or group endeavor. The church comes
before the Lord, gathered as one body. Armies do not have
soloists. An army made up of individual stragglers will not survive. No army will survive if each soldier is looking out only for
self. No battle can be won unless the soldiers experience a spiritual bond with one another.

Many Christians think they can run solo and call themselves Christians. No one can trust a soloist when a group effort is needed. Satan fools them into thinking that they need not belong to a local church. They believe they can watch sermons or worship on television and do their ministry on the job. But God calls us to be an army. There's no such thing as an army of one. Anyone who claims to believe in Jesus needs to be in God's army. Stop running solo because God wants an army. God doesn't hire mercenaries to do His work. Growing up in His strength means being a soldier in His army.

HIS STRENGTH, NOT OURS

When David was up against the Philistine (Goliath), he said, "And all this assembly shall know that the LORD saveth not with sword and spear: for the battle is the LORD's, and he will give you into our hands" (1 Samuel 17:47). Now that's speaking with confidence. David knew, like Paul knew, and like we should know, that the battle is not against flesh and blood. David knew the Philistine needed to know that God had the power. David  *In God's army, the victory is not ours, it belongs to the Lord.* was not confident in himself; rather, he was confident in the Lord. When we stand, we can speak like we ought, confident in the One who has all power.

In God's army, the victory is not ours; it belongs to the Lord. David spoke confidently because he knew that he was not the one fighting the battle, but the Lord was. The very first verse in this passage (Ephesians 6:10-20) tells us to be strong in the

Lord and in the power of His might, not our own might. He gave us the spiritual cloth-ing to go into bat-tle. God has not sent His army ill-prepared. In God's

... growing up to the Head in His strength means always giving God the glory.

army and with God's armor, the victory is His. He is victori-ous by the power of His might. God will always have the vic-tory. No matter how things appear at any point in battle, God will have the victory. Some battles are heavy. Sometimes there are casualties. But God always wins in spiritual warfare. Therefore, growing up to the Head in His strength means always giving God the glory.

STAND

Finally, Paul tells us simply to stand. I'm convinced that God realized our success is primarily about defense and not offense. Being an offensive-minded person, I had to study this a long while. Christian offense is built primarily on defense. That's why he says, "Just stand."

I am reminded of the late 1950's and early 1960's, during the Civil Rights era, when we were in Alabama, trying to break down barriers of segregation. We didn't fight back then. Even with dogs biting at us and water being put on us, we just stood. In the face of our White brothers' anger and hatred, we stood. Confronting all they had to throw at us, we stood. It takes a spe-cial strength to stand in the face of battle. It took His strength to keep us from retaliating during the Civil Rights movement.

In battle, it says a lot if you are the last one standing. The last man standing in a prize fight is the winner. The army standing at the end of battle has the victory. Put on the

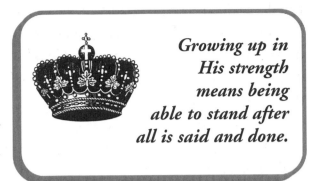

Growing up in His strength means being able to stand after all is said and done.

whole armor of God and just stand. I used to coach football. The way that I learned to teach boys to win football games was, first of all, to have a good defense. A team can have a powerful offense, yet be defeated because the opposing team had an effective defense. The best offense is a always good defense. Therefore, just stand. Whatever you do, just stand. Put on the whole armor of God and just stand. Growing up in His strength means being able to stand after all is said and done.

APPLICATION

How does growing up to the Head in His strength affect the spiritual and numerical growth of the church? This question can be answered by explaining how many churches and church members either are not fully dressed for spiritual warfare or have misused the equipment God has given due to a lack of training.

First, some churches and church members are not fully dressed in His armor. They may want to pick and choose which portions of God's armor they want to wear. They are not fully dressed! A church that is not fully dressed will avoid dealing with some issues that arise within the body.

Many are missing the breastplate of righteousness. Their vital organs are exposed and vulnerable to the demons of this world. Some who have devoted their lives to spiritual warfare have observed that demons enter us when we have been made vulnerable. The breastplate keeps us from being vulnerable because our vital organs are protected from evil by His righteousness. There are many people living with demons. They are not the "Exorcist" style demons. Rather, they are the evil spirits which rob us of the joy which Christ intended for us. Demons of fear, faithlessness, jealousy, envy, hatred, anger, greed, lust, and the like can plague our lives and rob us of life in the fullness of His strength.

Second, many churches have not trained their members to use what God has equipped them with; therefore, the body's potential is stunted. Many church members are carrying around a sword, the word of God, and don't know what to do with it. The army does not send a soldier to battle without training him on the proper use and care of his weaponry. The church lets soldiers go into the world all the time with a weapons and no training. They do not provide relevant Bible study. There is no training concerning how our actions and activities in the church relate to the words God has given us in the Bible.

Some churches want to use the edge of the sword that

> *A member or a church that only has a one-sided sword is dangerous and inadequately equipped.*

cuts, but not the one that helps and heals. Some keep the cutting edge of the sword razor sharp while letting the healing edge grow dull or even rusty. These churches are long on criticism and condemnation and short on love, forgiveness and healing. It often seems that churches and denominations which emphasize all of the "don'ts" in life have more people in their ranks doing the don'ts than other churches. A member or a church that only has a one-sided sword is dangerous and inadequately equipped.

There are Christians in churches all over this country who have been doing things for years and have no idea why. Some members don't know why we take communion, why we baptize, why we praise, why we ordain deacons

Growing up to the Head in His strength means teaching the congregation appropriate use of the sword (Word).

and preachers, why we say "amen," why we go and tell others about Jesus. Others carry the sword and think that something will happen simply because they are carrying it in their hands. Some think that carrying a big sword makes a difference. Some believers carry a big Bible with them because they believe it makes others think that they are really serious about God's Word. Those are the religious people Jesus told us to watch out for in Matthew 6:1-18—people who do things to be seen by others, not to please God. If the congregation is properly trained to use the sword, the church will grow. If the congregation is not properly trained to use the sword, not only will the church experience no spiritual growth, it may actually decline numerically. The sword cuts long and short. Growing up to the Head in His strength means teaching the congregation the appropriate use of the sword (Word).

God has given us all the equipment needed to win the victory. Churches that are able to equip members in the proper use of this equipment will be growing churches. There is nothing more frustrating than having a piece of equipment that you do not know how to use. People in the world are frustrated. They don't have the equipment and probably don't even know it exists. But some Christians in the church are frustrated, too. They have the equipment and don't know how to use it. The soldiers in God's army who are adequately equipped and knowledgeable are a powerful force. They cannot be defeated because God cannot be defeated. Church members and congregations who are growing up to His Head in strength know how to use the equipment God has given all believers.

A local church can be viewed as a battalion. Each battalion may have a special gift or responsibility. Some churches may be strongest in evangelism while some may be strongest in community ministry. Some churches may be strongest in helping families stay together in difficult times, and still others may be strongest in worship and praise. But if all these churches would function cooperatively, using the battalion model to serve in God's army, all churches would grow. People would be converted. Lives would be changed, renewed and victorious. Church members and congregations who have grown up in His strength don't underestimate the enemy. Members, new and long-term alike, need help to learn how to use the equipment they received when they accepted Christ.

FOR STUDY AND REVIEW

Chapter Ten
Growing Up to the Head in His Strength

1. What does it mean to dress for spiritual success?

2. List the six pieces of clothing which make up the whole armor of God? Which pieces are offensive weapons and which are defensive weapons?

   (1) _____

   (2) _____

   (3) _____

   (4) _____

   (5) _____

   (6) _____

3. A Christian is _____ without the _____ of God.

4. What is spiritual "dressing down"? How will it affect a Christian's ability to grow up to the Head in His strength?

5. Complete the following Scripture passage: "Sanctify them through thy _____: thy word is _____" (John 17:17). How is truth related to God's strength?

6. "I want to be like Mike" is a very popular slogan in the sports world. Write a similar slogan which should reflect every Christian's desire.

7. The helmet of _____ is used to protect the soldier's head. Why is it important to protect this part of the body?

8. Shoes are a sign of readiness. To grow up to the Head in His strength, what are some conditions a soldier must be ready to confront during spiritual warfare?

9. What is a double-edged sword? What would be the result of a single-edge sword on one with a dull side?

Growing Up in His Word

Read through the Book of Ephesians again, taking a closer look at each chapter. Choose the primary points you believe God is expressing in each chapter. What reason can you determine for the order in which Paul wrote the Book of Ephesians?

Growing Up Together

1. A church must rely on His strength for church growth. However, what other types of things should a local church do which does not constitute them "working in their own strength"?

2. What type of training does your church provide for soldiers in this spiritual battle? Is the training adequate? How can it be improved?

Grow Up to the Head!

1. Check your armor! Periodically, every soldier's equipment must pass inspection. If Christ were presently looking at your equipment, what would He see and what do you believe would be His comments?

2. The whole armor of God is not something to be removed at the end of the day. Visualize yourself dressed for spiritual success. Write down why it would be difficult to do anything except *stand* when you are fully armed!

GROWING UP TO THE HEAD

Living on Your Tiptoes

Living on your tiptoes means continuously stretching and striving to grow up to the fullness of Christ, the perfect Head of All in All. It is as if God has put a crown above

> *It is as if God has put a crown above every believer's head and has admonished us to get on our tiptoes so our head can wear the crown.*

every believer's head and has admonished us to get on our tiptoes so our head can wear the crown. Yet the crown is always a little higher than we can reach. Therefore, we get on our tiptoes in an effort to make contact with the crown. Living on our tiptoes means daily trying to grow up unto Him who is the Head of our lives. The crown we tiptoe to reach is representative of the perfect, holy Christ. The crown represents He who has called us to live worthy of our calling.

Ephesians 4:1b states, "...I urge you to live a life worthy of the calling you have received" (NIV). What is the calling we have received? Specifically, this text is calling us to grow up in the unity of the body, the Church. Growing up in unity means that everything is connected: one body, one Spirit, one hope, one Lord, one faith, one baptism, one God and one Father of all. We are challenged to grow up in the unity of the body by expressing, preserving and affirming our spiritual unity. To fulfill the calling of worthiness, we must daily strive to keep the body connected. We must live on our tiptoes.

We must live on our tiptoes because, apart from Christ, we are not perfect. By being in Christ we find perfection. We live on our tiptoes trying to grow up to the crown of love and peace. We live on our tiptoes trying to grow up in the fullness of His knowledge. We live on our tiptoes trying to grow up to our calling to pray and praise. We live on our tiptoes trying to grow up in reconciliation in the oneness of His love. We live on our tiptoes attempting to reach the high calling of stewardship, giving and service. We live on our tiptoes in an attempt to grow up to the fulfillment of His purpose, His ableness, and His power.

His love for us can never be repaid. His grace escapes our worthiness. We try to grow up to it, but we forever find ourselves wanting. His crown eludes us. We tiptoe, we stretch, we even jump, but the crown of love, mercy, grace and holiness is too high. Don't be alarmed! A tiptoe existence is only temporary. God has promised that one day we will be like Him. On that day, tiptoe living will be over.

Ephesians 4:13 states, "Till we all come ... into a perfect man, unto the measure of the stature of the fullness of Christ." Thank God for the "till." Until tells us that one day, tiptoe living will come to an end. God has promised that we will reach the crown, the Head. God's Word declares, "It doth not yet appear what we shall be: but we know that, when he shall appear, we shall be like him; for we shall see him as he is" (1 John 3:2). We will grow up. We will see Him face-to-face. We will have a glorified body like His. We will have a crown. We will grow up to the Head.

BIBLIOGRAPHY

Frankl, Viktor E. *Man's Search for Meaning*. Boston: Beacon Press, 1992.

Hemphill, Ken. *The Antioch Effect: Eight Characteristics of Highly Effective People*. Nashville: Broadman & Holman Publishers, 1994.

Johnson, Barbara. *Stick a Geranium in Your Hat and Be Happy!* New York: Inspirational Press, 1990.

King, Stephen. "Rita Hayworth and the Shawshank Redemption." In *Different Seasons*. New York: Viking Press, 1982.

Malloy, John T. *Dress for Success*. New York: Warner Books, 1975.

Meyer, Joyce. *If Not for the Grace of God*. Tulsa, Oklahoma: Harrison House, 1995.

Sheldon, Charles M. *In His Steps* (abridged). Uhrichsville, Ohio: Barbour and Company, Inc., 1995.

Sjogren, Steve. *Conspiracy of Kindness*. Ann Arbor, Michigan: Servant Publications, 1993.